The Ultimate Guide to Business Insurance

Scott Louis Cooper
CDR. USNR-Ret.

Fariba Cooper
Contributing Author

Publisher: Efluential Publishing, a division of Efluential Marketing LLC

The Key to Scott Cooper is his service. I TRUST HIM. He is always there. Insurance company is insurance company. Scott is who I trust and I value his opinion. If he doesn't have an answer to a question he will find the answer for me. He is my insurance doctor. Always gives me my choices and lets me make a decision. He really cares.

Michael Anderson
Chez Jay restaurant
client for 30 years

I knew Scott when he owned his restaurant in Glendale prior to the change of his career to a restaurant insurance broker. It was reassuring that he came from that environment and understood the restaurant industry and our struggles as an owner. In addition Scott is persistent and conscientious and always anticipates our needs, he has responded accordingly with the right insurance and the right limits, never over-insuring or under-insuring.

In 28 years that we have had our business insurance with him we started with two locations and now we have over 12 locations. Over many years we have had our share of claims and Scott's commitment and expertise to restaurants and his personal involvement in claims had made the insurance carriers take great care of our needs with the claims.

Joe DeSantis
Multi-State unit operator (L.A Italian Kitchen)

Scott has been helping protect my business for years. This is an amazing, easy to read guide that every restaurant owner should get. This book will no doubt save many businesses in the food and beverage industry from serious financial losses on lawsuits.

Adelmo Zarif, owner Cicada Restaurant

A few years ago Scott convinced me to that I was unprotected and needed to purchase EPLI coverage, I first thought he was crazy. Within a couple of months we had a very large claim and a few claims since then. Scott has a great instinct and he is someone you can really trust. He takes excellent care of us. The claims payout was over $550,000.

Toby Idol
Pacific Dinning Car (Established 1921)

"The reason I have done business for a long time with Scott ~~and~~ even though many other Brokers have approached me is that Scott treats me more like a friend. It is a relationship. He gives me the best honest advice and treats it like it's his own business. Even if the premium is higher, which it is not (much lower), I would continue doing business with him."

Paolo Simeone
Multi-Unit Operator throughout Los Angeles
Trastevere
La Piazza
Al Mare

"Scott has provided many years of sage guidance in both insurance and business matters. His business background and acumen have proven to be invaluable and has given us the peace of mind to know we are in the best hands available."

Robert Singer
Proprietor over 25 Years
C&O Trattoria
C& O Cucina
Marina Del Rey

There's a comfort in doing business with someone who specializes in your industry and keeps you informed of the new laws and regulations affecting our industry. Scott is smart, but his warmth and humor makes it a pleasure to work with him, too.

Lee and Marti Spencer
Warehouse Restaurant Marina Del Rey
Smokehouse Restaurant Burbank, Established 1946

Contents

Dedication xi

With Utmost Gratitude xv

Introduction xvii

About the Author xxi

CHAPTER 1
Employment Practice Claims, A Restaurant Owner's
Nightmare 1

Sexual harassment
Wrongful termination
Discrimination
Americans with Disabilities Act
Checklist

CHAPTER 2
Is Health Care Reform Healthy for Your Business?
Facts and Myths – What You Don't Know Can and
Will Hurt You! 23

Determining your number of full time equivalents
(FTEs)
Legal requirements for small and large employers
Which employees must be offered coverage and when
Reporting requirements for employees
Health plans minimum required coverage and
"affordability"
IRS penalties for non-compliance
What if I own more than one small business?
Transitional relief
Grandfathered and Grandmothered plans
IRS reporting requirements

CHAPTER 3

Worker's Comp or Retaliation?
Control Claims and Lower Your Premium! 37

Property and Liability coverage
Claims
Employee Dishonesty
Admitted vs. Non Admitted
Assault and battery
Equipment failure
Delivery
Checklist
Glossary of workers comp insurance terms

CHAPTER 4

Understanding Business Insurance Liability and
Managing Your Risk?.. 49

Worker's comp rates
Understanding your Ex-mod
Safety program
Claims
Audits
Employee classification
Checklist

CHAPTER 5

Cyber-liability, the New Information Highway Robbery,
Data Breach, and Identity Theft - If You Think Credit
Card Companies are Protecting You in Case of Fraud,
Think Again! 89

Data breach
Identity theft
You are responsible
Check list

CHAPTER 6
  High Risk Outside Your Premises - The
  Hidden Dangers.. 95

      Hired auto
      Non-owned Auto
      Catering
      Valet
      Checklist

CHAPTER 7
  Costly Natural and Not So Natural Disasters – Are
  You Prepared? 103

      Loss of income
      Riots
      Earthquakes, hurricanes and floods oh my!!
      Claim

CHAPTER 8
  Your Expert Team - Interviews with Business &
  Industry Experts 111

CHAPTER 9
  Valuable Insurance and Risk Management Resources 125

CHAPTER 10
  My Promise to You.. 127

DEDICATION

Dedicated to my Dad
M. Cooper & Sons

It was my favorite thing to do with my dad; going on a ride to visit his restaurant clients. He started to take me with him on calls when I was about 8 years old to restaurants, bars and clubs. I especially liked this Middle Eastern restaurant that had a belly dancing show. I loved watching the dancer do all sort of fascinating tricks with her belly including rolling a quarter up and down just using her stomach muscles.

Somewhere along the route my dad would say, "Remember Scotty, this will be your business one day. You will get to go visit them and take their orders." I was about 14 when I started to catch rides with some of his drivers to drop off their liquor order. All through high school I helped my dad whenever I could. As my dad was a wholesale liquor distributor, he even had some of the liquor named after us. Mine was liquor called Grand Louie after my middle name. We even had Coopers Vodka and Coopers Gin. Unfortunately, when I was still in college the liquor industry was deregulated under the Fair Trade Act, and it made it impossible to compete with the large warehouses. Dad was smart and sold his business before the law went into effect.

But, there was no more M .Cooper & Sons family business to pass down. After college, I became a commissioned US NAVY Officer that made my WWII combat veteran dad very proud. But, I always knew that one day I wanted to have my own business just like him. Being raised around the restaurant business created a natural desire in me to buy a restaurant to call my own in Glendale, California.

As much as I enjoyed it, it just wasn't the same as going out on those sales calls and visiting many different restaurant owners. But, it was a great and invaluable experience. I got to walk in the shoes of restaurant owners (not easy shoes to fill). There were the employee issues, dealing with the suppliers and purveyor, watching the food cost, and worrying about cash control when I wasn't there. One of my biggest frustrations I encountered while operating my restaurant was dealing with the three insurance agents I had that I never met. They never came to review my coverage, or even assist me with my claims. Well, I decided to sell my restaurant, but serve the restaurant owners with what seemed to be a shortage of caring professional restaurant insurance agents. I was Maurice Jay Cooper's son and the sales ability was running in my veins just like him.

Dad liked the idea, plus I already knew so many of my dad's clients that I could approach. One of my dad's first clients was a famous restaurant by the Santa Monica pier called *Chez Jay* operated by Alice which was Jay's mom. Alice and my dad became great friends. She always valued my dad's advice.

The restaurant was managed by Mike Anderson, now the owner of one the most famous landmark establishments in Santa Monica for over 50 years. Mike has trusted me and been my client and friend since the first day I became an agent with Farmers Insurance, and when I moved to become an independent insurance broker owning my own agency. That is not a relationship I have ever taken for granted. My dad was well known and respected in the industry for his integrity and good business sense always giving his advice to his restaurants and bars. I had big shoes to fill.

Found the Love of My Life...Lost My Life's Hero.

The year I got married is the year my new bride and I both became insurance agents. It was an emotional year being newlyweds, starting a new career and my dad was diagnosed with cancer. I lost him eight months later.

Today, as I drive to my clients all over the town, I still

remember all of my drives with my dad to his restaurant clients. Every street corner is filled with his stories. Now, when I take my son, Sean, to sales call with me, I always tell him whatever he decides to do in life, I know he will do great because he is a people person just like his Grandpa Jay.

WITH UTMOST GRATITUDE

I truly could not have done this without the help and support of my family, colleagues and staff.

To my life and business partner, Fariba; Your creativity and vision has been the foundation of this book. You are my true inspiration. Without you this book would have simply not happened.

To my beautiful kids Chaniel and Sean; your love is what drives me every day.

To our incredible expert colleagues; thank you for your continuous support and partnership with our agency and assisting our clients over the years. I truly value my relationship and friendship with each one of you

Keith; your expertise in Employment law and your dedication to our clients has been greatly appreciated. Your contribution to our Employment Practices Liability chapter has been invaluable.

Rob; you have simply mastered your field of benefits, Life and Disability. As always, together we will continue to provide the best benefit products to all our clients.

Mario; you are one of the few restaurant broker professionals I know of that is completely honest with your clients. Putting their benefits before your own is so admirable.

Jeff; your help with the research work for this book has been so appreciated. Thank you for your integrity and caring for this project.

To my amazing office staff, Marla, Annmarie, Jenna, Miriam, and Raquel; your hard work and dedication to our clients is what makes my day possible and beautiful. I could not ask for a better team.

To Cliff; you are a fantastic coach. Thank you for everything.

To Frieda; your friendship and wisdom is a blessing. Thank you.

To my clients, I owe the biggest gratitude for your loyalty and the privilege of allowing me to be your trusted adviser over the years.

--Scott

INTRODUCTION

I AM NOT A DOCTOR, but in my profession it is not uncommon to get a call after hours, or even in the middle of the night, and hear a panicked voice on the line.

"Scott, I just got a call from the fire department. My restaurant in Los Angeles is on fire. Who do I call? What do I do? I don't know the extent or the cause, but I am on my way over there!"

What this client forgot is that after eight years of being my client, when he gave the management of the restaurant to his newly college graduated son-in-law, the son-in-law decided to move the insurance package to another agent for a "savings" of just over $5,000.00 annually on his premium. He was so proud of his accomplishment. That was a big savings. OR WAS IT?

Unfortunately, my attempt to explain the grossly under-insured coverage on the building and his business personal property to the son-in-law was not successful. I even attempted to contact my client of eight years for his advice and involvement, but it was to no avail. He told me on more than one occasion that his son-in-law is in charge, and he has confidence in him.

Although their current agent wouldn't answer their emergency call until his office was open Monday morning after 9 am, I met with him at the location on Sunday morning mostly to advise him and give him moral support. Unfortunately, the insurance claim payoff was over a million and half dollars short on the building coverage. This restaurant never did reopen. If it can happen to him, it can happen to you.

I am once again their agent on their other locations and they are adequately covered.

Sadly, this scenario is not unusual. We have had many incidents where our restaurant owners are expanding to multiple locations, or sometimes they decide to partially or fully retire from everyday operation and delegate some of the responsibilities to the "pros" and do not oversee some of the crucial areas of their restaurant management. The bookkeeper, CPA, general manager, inexperienced son-in-law are making decisions on insurance, or have control of the checks, payrolls, bank cash deposits. It is imperative not to give over all control without proper systems for checks and balances, and appropriate insurance coverage (see chapter on employee dishonesty insurance page).

He said/She said

What happens when a girl's night out turns into your worst nightmare? When one young lady has a few drinks and the valet attendant decides to take advantage?

In the lawsuit my client received the young lady recalled being raped. The valet had a little different version. "She came on to me and offered her car." No one will ever know the truth.

"THE TRUTH"

Does the TRUTH even matter?

NO, I am sorry to disappoint you. In my 28 years of professional experience and expertise, the so called TRUTH is mostly irrelevant. Just the cost of legal expenses alone can be devastating to a restaurant owner. And, if it even makes it to court proceedings, after legal counsels put their versions and interpretations on it, it will not resemble in any shape or form the TRUTH.

So what does matter?

Cover your "A$$ets"

Do your own due diligence, anticipate and always make sure

you are adequately covered in areas where there is the greatest exposure. Above all, don't be penny wise and dollar foolish. Look for your insurance agent to be a trusted expert in restaurant insurance and don't stop simply at who's offering the lowest premium. The real cost is when you have a claim.

In this case, even though the valet company was an independent company hired by our client the restaurant was named in the lawsuit. We made sure our client was added as additional insured and they had a current and comprehensive policy.

Total claim paid out? Sorry, it is still ongoing. There are only two things for sure.

1. It will be BIG!

2. My client is well protected.

By the way, can you imagine the cost of defending yourself in a case like this? If it can happen to him it can happen to you.

Over the years, I have worked with hundreds of businesses and restaurant owners from small cafés to very large multiple franchise owners. I have helped international clients with every ethnic food you can imagine from traditional burger places to some of the most famous chefs in the industry. I discovered several important facts that most restaurateurs have in common.

I have been asked a lot of similar great valid questions. But, there are also a lot of very important questions that clients sometimes don't know they should be asking.

This book is written to help you identify some of the risks your business faces and what you can do to minimize your exposure. It is laid out in a simple and easy to follow format. There are seven chapters dedicated to different areas of insurance that can impact your business in a profound way.

Each chapter has an introduction, frequently asked questions clients do ask, and also questions they should be asking. There is also a check list of specific action items you can do to make sure your business is protected. I am also including some actual true claims examples.

Chapter eight contains powerful information; interviews with experts. In this chapter, we have conducted interviews with colleagues that we have had the privilege of working with in some cases over 20 years. Their valuable knowledge has helped our clients, and we know they will benefit you, your restaurant management, asset protection, asset allocation, loss prevention and reduction, and many other areas.

Chapter nine is dedicated to resources that can be beneficial to the operation of your restaurant. Each one has a link to our website for your easy accessibility.

Please keep in mind that as we update new information and resources, we are constantly updating our website.

Our first chapter is dedicated to the biggest trend in our industry, and where there is major potential for a catastrophic law suit.

ABOUT THE AUTHOR

Scott Louis Cooper, CDR, USNR-RET.

Scott Cooper, a respected insurance and risk consultant, is an authority in the hospitality insurance industry and President of Cooper's Insurance Agency, Inc. He has been an insurance instructor at UCLA, a guest speaker and lecturer, author, and expert witness.

Scott is a broker-affiliate of Professional Insurance Associates, one of the top 50 agencies in the United States and licensed in all 50 states. His expertise in the restaurant and hospitality field has earned him the respect of national companies, colleagues, affiliates, and clients nationwide. Scott, along with his business partner and wife Fariba, own and operate their business in beautiful sunny Southern California, and continue to have the honor of serving their clients for over 28 years.

CHAPTER 1

Employment Practice Claims, A Restaurant Owner's Nightmare

It never ceases to amaze me some of the claims I hear from my clients. They get angry and frustrated, but most of all they feel betrayed. One of my long time clients had a story that, to this day, perplexes us even in our industry. If it can happen to him, it can happen to you.

"Every day when I got to my restaurant, I noticed a homeless guy sitting in my adjacent parking lot. Of course, I offered him food. One day, I asked him if he wanted to make some extra cash by helping to monitor the parking lot for our restaurant. He did a great job.

After a few months, I hired him as a helper in the kitchen. I gave him some money to clean up and get some clothes. I even paid for his rent for few months until he got on his feet. He was very appreciative and worked hard.

Within a year, he asked me if I could advance him some money to buy a used trailer so he didn't have to share a room and have some privacy. I was doing a good deed and I felt great about it.

Well, everyone at the restaurant accepted him as one of their own. I knew he had made some friends with some of his coworkers, so when they were playing around and joking with each other no one made notice of it. The next day, he came to my office and said one of the other kitchen employees pulled his pants down and he was very upset over it. I was very busy at the time and didn't immediately address the issue. A week later, I received a major lawsuit for sexual harassment."

This claim was submitted to his insurance company under his

EPLI coverage. Over $230,000.00 was spent to defend this unproven allegation. If it can happen to him, it can happen to you.

Sometimes, employee's band together as a class and all file one lawsuit. Strength in numbers I guess. This happened to some of my clients who were recently involved in a huge class action where managers said they should not be exempt from overtime pay because they spend more than half their time doing things that are not managerial. Along the same lines, I have a client who had a 30 year employee file a claim for overtime he felt he was due for all 30 of the years he was employed. Longevity won't protect you. Being a "good guy" won't protect you. Any seemingly small, insignificant thing can suddenly make a loyal, trusted employee turn on you. This same employee filed a worker's comp claim for repetitive injury sustained over the 30 years. If it can happen to him, it can happen to you.

Can a pit bull be a working dog? According to the Americans with Disabilities Act, YES. I had a long time client ask one of his customers to dine on the patio with his pit bull instead of inside the restaurant. An extremely accommodating request one would think. But, the customer claimed the pit bull was an service animal, despite the fact he was not trained or certified, and sued under the ADA. If it can happen to him, it can happen to you.

Employment Practice Liability Insurance (EPLI) coverage is an essential part of your total insurance plan. Because employment law is constantly changing and extremely complex, I have enlisted the help of an expert to write this chapter. Keith Fink has handled a wide variety of cases in state and federal courts throughout the United States with the majority of cases all over California. His experience as a labor and employment lawyer is extensive. He has his entire career defended employers in wrongful termination, discrimination, harassment and wage and hour lawsuits. In addition to being hired by individual businesses, Mr. Fink has been panel counsel for various EPLI carriers. He is a highly sought after trainer in the area of sexual harassment, conducts independent sexual harassment investigations, and assists in revising and drafting employee handbooks and other personnel forms. Mr. Fink opened his own firm over a decade ago, and is an adjunct professor at UCLA and Southwestern University School of Law. I recently attended a local Thai Chamber of Commerce meeting at midnight where 197 restaurant owners came to hear Mr. Fink speak on EPLI and measures to protect a business. I posed what I have found to be some of the most important EPLI questions to Mr. Fink.

The Questions Clients Mostly Ask

1. What is EPLI and what does it cover?

EPLI is an acronym for Employment Practices Liability Insurance. While this product has now been on the market for at least fifteen years many brokers are unfamiliar with the details of the product and importance of it to a business owner. EPLI offers insurance coverage not provided in other insurance policies (e.g. workers compensation, CGL) against a myriad of claims brought against a business including to the following:

- Sexual Harassment
- Wrongful Termination

- Constructive Discharge (this is noted separately from wrongful termination as many business owners do not understand that the law allows an employee to quit and still file a wrongful discharge lawsuit. To do this an employee must allege he was subjected to intolerable conditions and that the employer knew of the intolerable conditions.)

- Discrimination (these claims are based on race,

religion, national origin, age, sexual orientation, pregnancy, marital status and disability to name just a few).

- Family Medical Leave Act. (FMLA)

- Defamation

- Invasion of Privacy

- Third party claims (such as a vendor who makes a claim based on the actions of an employee or a customer who makes a claim against the employer) under the right EPLI policy.

2. What is the biggest trend of lawsuits that face business owners today?

An endless rise in wage and hour lawsuits with a focus if possible on the "lottery" class action suits.

3. Why do I need EPLI?

You need EPLI because it is inevitable that your business is going be sued and when it is only one thing is certain: you will be out of pocket a significant amount of money no matter the result of the lawsuit. Many employers who have never been sued think they are somehow immune from a lawsuit. Nothing could be further from the truth. The reality is they have just been lucky to date and that the "shoe" is inevitably going "to drop" on the business in the form of some employee claim. The types of claims that are covered by EPLI are rising dramatically with the most coming from California which is a state with a byzantine labor code that is ever changing and virtually impossible for any business owner to keep up with. In certain industries such as food and beverage lawsuits are coming not only directly from employees with private attorneys but from the government as well. The DOL (Department of Labor) has ramped up its efforts to enforce wage and hour laws and has become aggressive in pursuing federal actions against restaurants for failure to pay the minimum wage and overtime. No matter the type of claim filed against an employer the cost to defend an action is very expensive. This is why a candid lawyer will tell you that once you have been sued you have lost even if you win. If you "win" the case in addition to spending countless man hours dealing with discovery you will have spent on average $150,000 defending the case. If you lose the case on top of the money you paid your lawyer you will be responsible to pay the plaintiff's award and depending on the claim ALL of the attorneys fees the plaintiff incurs. An average employment suit fully litigated with a verdict for the plaintiff will likely be in mid six figures when all fees/costs/awards are totaled and if the case is a bad one in the seven figures. "The Price is Right" TV show recently lost a single plaintiff pregnancy case for close to nine million dollars (the trial court did take away the verdict). This should underscore that every employee is a potential million dollar silver bullet to a company. No business owner should forget that if a case gets to a jury trial the employer is more likely not to win. The jury will certainly not be a jury of the business owner's peers. The jury will likely be made up of hard working employees just like the plaintiff and arguments such as the employee was "at-will" and the employer didn't need a reason to fire the employee will be ignored at best by the jury and most likely will inflame the jurors against the employer.

4. What are the most common types of EPLI claims?

The vast majority of claims are some sort of wrongful termination claim. After wrongful termination claims the majority of claims are for harassment or retaliation. In recent years wage and hour claims have been increasing but those claims are probably not in an everyday sense EPLI claims if all that is provided is a small sublimit on a policy for defense fees. In the hospitality industry there is a cottage industry of lawsuits based on violations of the ADA (Americans with

Disabilities Act) or parallel state law. These ADA lawsuits are almost impossible to win and are very expensive to litigate. The laws governing accessibility are complex and many business owners who lease assume the landlord has complied with state and federal accessibility laws or will indemnify them in litigation. There are plaintiff's attorneys who have disabled clients go from establishment to establishment seeking minor violations of the ADA. Very few people have the legal bullets like Clint Eastwood to fight these lawsuits. Mr. Eastwood's long battle in connection with an ADA suit against his Mission Ranch hotel in Carmel should serve as a good example of the minor violations that can give rise to such suits and that the plaintiff is not required to give a business owner advance notice of a structural defect before filing suit.

5. California is an "At Will" State so am I still liable for wrongful termination?

The truth is being an at-will state means very little in terms of having any legal protection from an employment lawsuit. There are so many exceptions to the at-will doctrine that the exceptions have swallowed the rule. Take for example a female employee who has worked at a cafe for twenty years starting as a hostess and then promoted to a waitress and then promoted to a general manager. After twenty years working at the cafe her salary has become high given yearly raises. If she is let go for no reason or even for a legitimate reason such as the business can no longer afford her she can easily plead around the at-will doctrine. Because she is a woman she can claim she was fired based on her gender. If she is over forty she can claim she was fired because of her age. If she recently posted on her Facebook page she likes women and the owner is a Facebook friend and a conservative she could claim she was fired because of her sexual orientation. Of course having worked for the cafe for twenty years she may be allowed to claim she had an implied in fact contract to be fired only for cause. If recently she complained about her belief that employees were not receiving all their wages she could claim her firing was retaliatory for raising this complaint. The exceptions to the at-will doctrine are endless.

6. Do any of my other policies cover EPLI like general liability or umbrella?

Most policies do not and have specific employment exclusions. There are some D and O (Directors and Officers liability) policies as well as Property and Liability Policies that have an inexpensive add-on option. These Liability policies provide very limited coverage and have small policy limits. The D and O option may have greater coverage and limits but an officer or director is likely to be very upset that his D and O coverage could be severely impacted from an employment suit.

7. My employees are like family, they won't make a claim.

When couples get divorced the breakup often leads to marital disputes over issues such as child and spousal support. When family members are left out of wills there is often extensive probate litigation. When family members are partners and the partnership breaks up this leads to business litigation. I tell my clients in business settings that like a marriage "there is amity now but there may be enmity later." An employee once he is fired has many reasons to make a claim. First, if the employee actually thinks he "is family" he is going to be angry that he was thrown out of the family business and left with nothing. Second, an employee's subjective perception about his performance is usually vastly different then an employers. If an employee believes he was fired unjustly he may seek to file a lawsuit. Third, the discharged employee usually sees only a financial upside in filing a lawsuit. Other then the small payment from the EDD the employee who cannot find another job or cannot find a job making the same money as the job they had can get the money they lost from being fired by a lawsuit. The discharged employee will always be able to find a lawyer to take his case on a contingency fee basis meaning the cost to the employee to sue an employer is nothing. Finally, the longer someone has been with you and the more they feel like family means the more likely you are to get sued and face a bad outcome. Consider the employee who works for a company for twenty years and is fired. This employee is now in his forties or fifties. It will likely be impossible for him ever to find another job paying the same money. This employee will be a sympathetic plaintiff everyone likes for a variety of reasons. The elderly employee may seem like every jurors grandparent. The jurors may feel it is just wrong after so many years to be fired for the reason proffered by the employer.

8. If I have a family operated business, do I still need EPLI?

Absolutely and perhaps more so then if your business wasn't a family operated one. Family operated businesses tend to be more informal in keeping records and complying with some of the more seemingly trivial labor laws. Recently ethnic owned family restaurants have been targeted for wage and hour lawsuits not by the family members but by the few non family members working as busboys and dishwashers.

9. Is EPLI required by law?

No, however homeowners insurance isn't required by law either unless you have a mortgage but nobody in their right mind would think about going without homeowners insurance. The rather minimal premium payment for both homeowners insurance and EPLI makes both bargains given the financial devastation that can occur if an event occurs triggering the applicability of such coverage. Quite possibly the chances of a business being wiped out from an employee lawsuit are greater than the chances of a flood, fire or other damage to a home.

10. Can I pick the Labor Attorney of my choice to represent me?

It depends. Generally you cannot because the vast majority of carriers have arrangements with a few law firms that serve as panel counsel for the carrier. If you believe that lawyers are not interchangeable and want to insure you get a lawyer with extensive employment experience then you should seek an endorsement that allows a certain law firm to defend your company if a claim is made or seek a policy that gives the carrier the ability only to withhold consent if your selection of counsel will not work for a commercially reasonable rate (usually that paid by the carrier) and lacks sufficient years of practice as an employment attorney.

11. What should a business owner look for in counsel and what training can labor law counsel provide?

An experienced employment law attorney can help greatly on almost every human resource issue. If an employer communicates with experienced counsel, they can get guidance now to limit legal exposure and the communication is all subject to the attorney-client privilege. An experienced lawyer can tell you not only the law, but ways to document (or not) the incident, and ways to separate with the employee in a manner protecting against litigation (e.g. how to handle an EDD claim. It is generally a big mistake to contest such claims).

12. What are the benefits of "an ounce of prevention vs. a pound of cure"? When do you consult a labor law specialist counsel?

The benefits can be your entire financial future. Most issues require a five to ten minute call. Assuming an employer gets proper advice, a $50 phone call could save hundreds of thousands. For example, an employee goes out on worker's compensation leave, and during that leave an employer wants to fire that employee because all of a sudden the employer has determined the employee was a poor employee. This would be a costly and foolish decision that a smart lawyer would advise you against in a minute, and give you an alternative strategy.

13. If I comply with all labor laws, why do I need EPLI coverage?

For several reasons. First, you can get sued even if you have complied with every local, state and federal labor law. A plaintiff's attorney (unless they are simply looking to shake you down for a nuisance settlement) isn't looking to file a lawsuit that has no merit. However, a plaintiff's attorney almost always hears only your former employee's version of the "facts" before filing suit. The discussion between the attorney and the client is usually no longer than an hour before the attorney decides to take the employee's case. The employer's version of the facts are not known to the plaintiff's attorney. The employer's documents backing up the employment decision are not known to the attorney.

Second, you may have thought it wise to hire a PEO to handle your employment issues and while you complied with all the labor laws they did not. Your company will get sued as a joint employer and depending on your agreement with the PEO and the PEO's insurance you might be left funding the defense of the action.

Finally, this question assumes you have complied with all labor laws which is well-nigh impossible. For example, very few people thought that having unpaid interns would be found to be a violation of wage and hour laws. A few weeks ago an opinion over the interns on the movie the "Black Swan" provides analysis that will likely render most unpaid internships illegal. Another example is the typical family maid. Almost everybody pays their maid some flat monthly sum. No time records are kept. No itemized pay stub is kept. No overtime is paid. Each maid is a ticking wage and hour time bomb even though you think you're complying with all laws.

14. If I don't have EPLI insurance, can I be sued as individual?

You can always be named individually. The most likely and viable claims against an individual in the employment setting are for harassment and retaliation. There are also a myriad of common law claims where an individual can be named. Depending on whether the business has properly used a corporate form an individual can be named as the employer. This routinely happens with smaller end restaurants.

The Questions Clients Should be Asking

1. What is the financial impact of a wage and hour lawsuit to the business owner?

A wage and hour lawsuit can be devastating to a business. EPLI policies do not cover judgments in such suits and fewer and fewer are even offering defense coverage these days. Defense fees alone on a single plaintiff wage and hour case are enough to wipe out a restaurant's profit in a year. It is imperative for today's business owner to familiarize himself or herself with all applicable state, local, and federal wage and hour laws and reporting requirements and to maintain strict compliance. Whenever possible, EPLI coverage should be obtained from a company that does offer limited wage and hour defense coverage.

2. What is Third Party and ADA claims?

Third party claims arise from lawsuits usually in one of two ways. First, an employee can claim that someone who does not work for the company has violated the employee's rights. For example, if a hostess at a restaurant is harassed every time the vendor for the cleaning company comes to deliver the cleaned table cloths and you are told about this and don't do anything then you could be liable for creating a hostile work environment. Second, customers can sue a business for actions done by an employee of the business. For example, if a customer is refused service because of his race then the customer has a civil rights suit. Both Papa John's and Chic Fil A recently were sued by customers when their employees made derogatory remarks about Asian customers. ADA claims refer to claims based on violations of the Americans with Disabilities Act.

3. What is the difference between exempt and non-exempt (hourly) employees?

The difference means a lot of money if the classification is incorrect. The direct answer is the terms refer to job classifications for employees and the exemption from minimum wage and overtime payments. Both federal law (FLSA) and state law apply to the proper determination. The reality is most employees are non-exempt. The employer must prove the employee meets a professional, executive or administrative exemption to avoid paying minimum wage and overtime. The biggest mistake is thinking a job title determines an employee's classification. Wrong. Simply calling a secretary an executive assistant doesn't make her exempt. The focus is usually on the employee's duties and whether the duties include the exercises of discretion and independent judgment. Employers also make the mistake in thinking paying someone a salary makes them exempt from overtime.

4. How do I reduce the possibility of an EPLI claim?

The number one way is treat employees you are firing with dignity. The essence is to be empathetic with them and try and offer as much assistance as you can to help them transition. You should always avoid slamming or crucifying an employee verbally when you're letting the employee go. The next way is not to fight the employee when he is seeking unemployment benefits. Finally you should get a signed enforceable release if you're giving a severance. If the employee is over forty you'll have to comply with the OWBPA (Older Workers Benefit Protection Act).

In terms of wage and hour suits, an audit should be done on each and every employee to determine if the employee is being properly classified. If an employer can avoid misclassification if a worker either as non-exempt or as an independent contractor, then the employer has cut off many difficult to defend claims. Adequate time records should be kept for every worker. This protects against a lawsuit where in the absence of records, the employee distorts the amount of hours worked. An employer should have a well written arbitration agreement. While not to be used in a reflexive manner, the process of arbitration is a pretty good bet to insure against a run-away jury verdict. An employer should purchase EPLI insurance, and if possible, pay extra for choice of counsel.

5. How does the EPLI claim process work?

Once an employer receives a "claim" (usually an administrative complaint, demand letter or lawsuit) the employer must tender it to the carrier. This can be done by sending it to the broker or directly to the carrier. The carrier will review the claim, appoint defense counsel and within a certain period of time provide a coverage opinion.

6. What procedures do I need in place for a new hire?

Many if not most lawsuits can be avoided simply by not hiring an employee who is likely to be a bad employee or is likely to sue you. To that end it is vital an employer conduct a background check on the applicant and conduct a face to face interview with the applicant.

While not required by law the following new hire documents should all be in place: (a) arbitration agreement; (b) sexual harassment policy with a grievance mechanism tailored to your business; (c) at-will document; (d) employee handbook.

7. What are the best practices for documentation before and after incidents?

This is a difficult question and depends upon the type of incident being investigated. For standard performance issues, it is a good practice to have copies of the deficient work (e.g. a memorandum with spelling and grammar errors), and an employee-signed performance review acknowledging they have been apprised of their performance issues. It is a mistake to document anything using a progressive discipline type form where the employee is told there are many "rivers to cross" before final termination occurs. With harassment documentation, it is essential that a thorough, objective and neutral investigation be done. Documentation such as inappropriate e-mails should be attached to any write-up.

8. How often should I update my employee handbook?

You should review your handbook yearly and modify it to keep up with the changes in federal and your state's laws.

9. What training is required by the State of California?

Employers with fifty or more employees or contractors must provide at least two hours of interactive sexual harassment training to all supervisory employees. It also mandates these trainings occur every other year. Even if not required, though, it is strongly advised that employers with fewer than fifty employees also provide this training for their supervisors.

10. Is listing all my business entities on the EPLI application important?

Yes especially if you are trying to get a master EPLI policy that covers all your business where there is 51 percent or more common ownership. In any event failure to list a business entity could provide the carrier with an out in a coverage dispute with the entity omitted from the application.

11. Do I need to list my landlord as additional insured?

You should especially if your lease requires you to indemnify the landlord against claims that arise from your tenancy.

12. How do I choose the best EPLI policy for my business?

Work with an experienced broker that knows the product. Do not try and save pennies in analyzing what limits to purchase.

13. What information is required and what are the premiums based on? Are EPLI policies expensive?

An application is filled out, loss runs are required when an existing policy is in place and some carriers will require a current financial statement. The premiums for an EPLI policy are based on number of full-time employees, part-time employees, owners/officers, independent contractors and the claims experience of the business.

Policies can range from a few hundred dollars with minimum coverage, to thousands for a comprehensive policy with prior claims. The price depends on employee count and claim experience. The value of a good EPLI policy can save potentially hundreds of thousands of dollars in a lawsuit. The proper marketing by an independent agent can greatly lower premiums.

Checklist for Employment Law Issues and EPLI Policies:

___ Employee handbook is up to date and regularly reviewed by a labor attorney. All employees receive a copy and sign for receipt.

___ A training program is in place for management covering the areas of workplace law and sexual harassment (required 2 hours every 2 years if more than 50 employees).

___ Standard training is in place for new employees that includes distribution of the employee handbook, zero tolerance for harassment, and how to report incidents.

___ Employees are properly classified regarding exempt or non-exempt from overtime.

___ An electronic time keeping system is in place with enforcement of required meal and rest periods.

___ Facility is compliant with the Americans with Disabilities Act.

___ An EPLI policy is in force that includes defense coverage for wage and hour claims.

___ The EPLI policy is reviewed and all entities and individuals, as well as all locations are named in the policy and covered.

If I Have a Claim:

___ All initial and ongoing verbal threats and written notices have been forwarded to my insurance agent.

___ All employees are reminded not to discuss any incident with anyone other than my insurance agent, claims adjuster, and/or attorney assigned by my insurance company.

The following charts and graphs illustrate the historical trends in employment practice lawsuits and judgments 2005-2011:

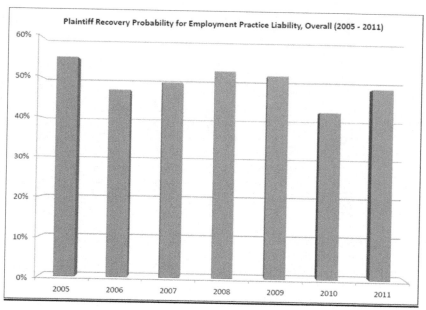

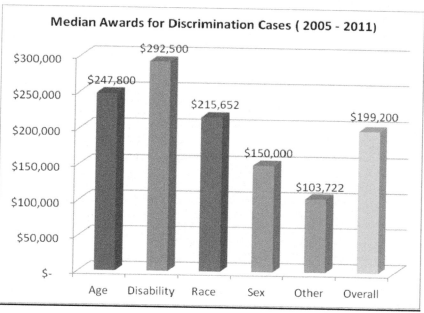

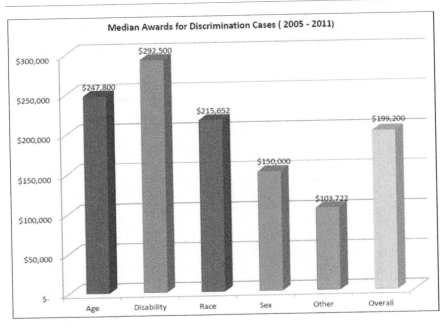

Median Awards for Discrimination Cases (2005 - 2011)

Distribution of Awards Age Discrimination Awards (2005 - 2011)

Award Range			Percentage
To		$ 4,999	3%
$ 5,000	-	$ 9,999	2%
$ 10,000	-	$ 24,999	2%
$ 25,000	-	$ 49,999	5%
$ 50,000	-	$ 74,999	10%
$ 75,000	-	$ 99,999	5%
$ 100,000	-	$ 249,999	23%
$ 250,000	-	$ 499,999	17%
$ 500,000	-	$ 749,999	9%
$ 750,000	-	$ 999,999	7%
$ 1,000,000	-	$ 1,999,999	10%
$ 2,000,000	-	$ 4,999,999	3%
$ 5,000,000	+		3%

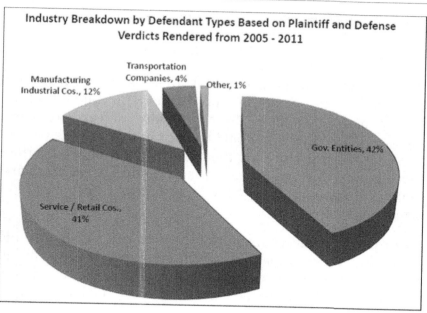

Industry Breakdown by Defendant Types Based on Plaintiff and Defense Verdicts Rendered from 2005 - 2011

- Manufacturing Industrial Cos., 12%
- Transportation Companies, 4%
- Other, 1%
- Gov. Entities, 42%
- Service / Retail Cos., 41%

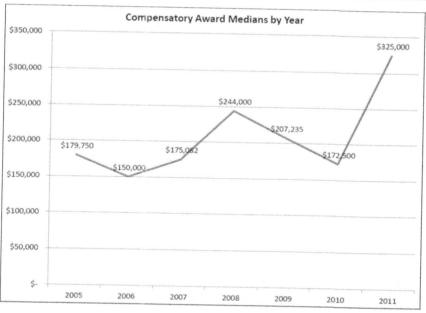

Compensatory Award Medians by Year

- $179,750
- $150,000
- $175,082
- $244,000
- $207,235
- $172,500
- $325,000

DIRECTORS AND OFFICERS INSURANCE

What is Directors and Officers Insurance?

Directors and Officers Liability Insurance coverage provides a company with financial protection for upper level management including directors and officers of your company. This coverage would be used in the case of a lawsuit resulting while performing their job responsibilities for their specific roles. A relevant comparison would be an Errors and Omissions policy, but geared specifically for executive management.

Directors and Officers Liability Insurance can usually include Employer Practices Liability which involves harassment and discrimination lawsuits, and is where the majority of liability lies for upper management. Also Fiduciary Liability can be purchased.

Directors and Officers Liability coverage is often confused with Errors and Omissions Liability coverage. These two types of coverage are not the same type of protection. The Errors and Omissions policy provides coverage for performance-related failures and negligence with respect to your products and services, not the performance and duties of management. Generally, it is a good idea to have both Directors and Officers Liability coverage, as well as Errors and Omission coverage.

When is Directors and Officers Needed?

When you assemble a board of directors, Directors and Officers Liability coverage becomes required. Investors, especially venture capitalists, will also require that you show evidence of Directors and Officers Liability Insurance as part of the conditions of investing funds within your company.

Also, having employees opens management up to employment practices lawsuits.

Why Do I Need Directors and Officers?

First, claims from stockholders, employees, and clients will be made at some point against the company, as well as against the directors of the company. Since a director can be held personally responsible for acts of the company, most directors and officers will demand Directors and Officers Liability coverage so that their personal assets are not at stake.

Second, investors and members of your board of directors will not be willing to risk their personal assets to serve as a corporate director or officer, no matter how emotionally invested they are in your company.

Last, employment practice suits make up the single largest area of claim activity under Director and Officer Liability policies. Over 50% of Directors & Officers claims are related to employee practices.

CHAPTER 2

Is Health Care Reform Healthy for Your Business?
Facts and Myths – What You Don't Know Can and Will Hurt You!

Bobby has been my client for over 15 years. When I first met him he would tell me how he only sees his commercial agent once a year. In the last 15 years Bobby's business has grown by leaps and bounds and he has worked very hard for this. Even with restaurant managers and a great staff he is a hands on operator. As successful as he is he works hard for his bottom line. He is very determined to keep his costs low. Bobby makes sure he is always informing his staff on all important updates and safety matters; to keep them safe and to keep his worker's comp rate low. He takes pride in the quality of his food; to reduce any food borne illness and to keep his reputation and service. In all areas Bobby is a hands-on kind of guy. Lately Bobby has been nervous. He has been calling me worried about Health Care Reform and how it will impact his business. How is he going to offer insurance and also keep track of the constant accounting and changes? How is that going to impact his bottom line? I realized at the beginning stages the Affordable Care Act would cause much frustration because it is so complicated. It has good intentions but it could potentially cause severe financial burden. If not done correctly the penalties alone can take a toll. Who has time for all this? "I am trying to run a business." said Bobby.

There is a lot of uncertainty. Even the experts don't know all the answers. We have been providing group and individual health products to our clients since our inception in 1985 but this is a whole other world....

Bobby and a lot of our other clients have been educating, or better yet confusing, themselves online. Some of the information out there is contradictory and it is constantly changing. The time lines, the rates, the government involvement, contribution, penalties...As always we are committed to finding the right answers. Tracking all the changes is an ongoing effort.

Yes we are committed to be by your side to make sense of it all. You are not alone. We are staying abreast of all new developments as they happen in this constantly changing landscape.

The following chapter offers and overview of some important factors to consider for health care reform.

Health Reform: A Guide for Employers

The Patient Protection and Affordable Care Act (PPACA) were signed and put in effect March 23, 2010. Amendments were made under the Health Care and Reconciliation Act on March 30, 2010. The Affordable Care Act (ACA) refers to the finalized and amended version of the law. This legislation will affect consumers and businesses as well as the management of health care for the vast majority of Americans.

Coopers Insurance has been providing health care products for consumers and businesses for nearly 30 years. This long established length of service in the insurance industry has provided experience and insight to determine the best methods of health care products at the best pricing. We developed this guide as an employer tool which can be used to better understand the changes that have taken place to health care laws. This information will help you take advantage of the new benefits and tax credits and will help you avoid costly penalties. The information in this chapter is current as of the date of publication. It will be updated as rules and timetables change.

Is the ACA going to increase my taxes?

While the majority of employers and employees won't pay any additional taxes under the ACA, there is an increase to the current Medicare part A tax for businesses and employees making over $200,000. There is also a requirement for employers with 50 full-time equivalent employees or more to offer health insurance to full-time workers or pay a penalty starting in 2015 / 2016.

What is a full-time equivalent employee?

ACA defines full-time status as employees with an average of 30 hours of service per week (130 hours of service per month). To figure out your full time equivalent employees take the total of all hours worked by all part-time employees for the month and divide by 120 to get the number of FTE employees. *Example: 20 PT employees with average of 15 hours of service per week = 1200 hours service per month divided by 120 = 10 FTE employees.* Add this number to the employees that meet the full time status description to get your total number of full time equivalent employees.

Sample Chart – ABC Company has about 38 full time and 25 part time (12-24 hours per week) employees:

Month	FT employees	Non-FT hours	Converted to FTEs	Equiv FTEs
Jan	38	1500	12.5	50.5
Feb	35	1700	14.2	49.2
Mar	38	1500	12.5	50.5
Apr	38	1600	13.3	51.3
May	39	1450	12.1	51.1
Jun	35	1800	15	50
Jul	35	1700	14.2	49.2

Aug	36	1750	14.6	50.6
Sep	34	1800	15	49
Oct	34	1800	15	49
Nov	34	1975	16.5	50.5
Dec	34	2000	16.7	50.7
		Sub Total		601.5
		Total Equivalent FTEs		50.1

Do I have to offer health coverage to my employees?

Come 2016, small businesses with over 50 full-time equivalent employees that choose not to provide insurance to full time employees, provide insurance that doesn't meet the minimum standards set forth by the act, or provide insurance where the cost to the employee exceeds 9.5% of family income (for employee only insurance) will have to pay a shared responsibility fee (penalty). For those with 100 or more FTE this starts in 2015. By 2016, employers with more than 50 FTEs will need to provide coverage to "substantially all" (95%) of their full-time employees and offer coverage for their children up to age 26. Spouse coverage is not required by the ACA.

For employees whose hours vary or are seasonal the ACA allows employers to use a standard measurement period of 3 to 12 months to determine their group size and who must be offered coverage. This is known as the "look back measurement method". Employers must use the same measurement period for all employees in the same category.

Employers with 200 or more employees must automatically enroll their employees in a qualified health plan but must give the employee adequate opportunity to "opt-out" if they do not want the employer provided coverage.

Do I have to provide coverage for independent contractors?

Under common law rules, anyone who performs services for you is your employee if you control what will be done and how it will be done. Changing an employee's status to 1099 from W-2 will not change the IRS' consideration of the employee's status when this principle is applied.

Do I have to provide coverage for owners and/or family members?

An owner is not counted if he/she is a sole proprietor, a partner in a partnership, a shareholder owning more than 2% of an S corporation or an owner of more than 5% of other types of corporations. Family members are not counted if they are children or grandchildren, siblings or step siblings, parents or grandparents, step parents, nieces or nephews, aunts or uncles, sons or daughters in law, fathers or mothers in law, or brothers or sisters in law. Owners and family members' wages and hours do not apply to the FTE calculation.

How much is the penalty if I do not offer coverage?

The penalty for businesses not offering their full-time workers a plan with the minimum essential coverage is outlined on the next few pages for employers with 50-99 FTE and for employers with 100+ FTE:

50-99 Employer Penalties 2015-2016

A" PENALTY 4980H (a)	B" PENALTY 4980H (b)
1. No offer of minimum essential coverage (MEC) 2. Trigger: FT employee gets Premium Tax Credit (PTC) from Exchange - No penalty for Medicaid enrollment 3. $2080* x all FT employees minus first 30 FT employees	1. Coverage is not affordable or does not provide minimum value 2. Trigger: FT employee gets Premium Tax Credit (PTC) from Exchange- No penalty for Medicaid enrollment 3. $3120* x each FT employee who gets PTC from Exchange; never higher than employer would have received for "A" Penalty.
✓ *Must offer to "all" FT employees* ✓ *Regulators defined "all" as 95% (all but greater of 5% or 5 FT)* ✓ *For 2015, no penalty* ✓ *Important to prepare in 2014 & 2015 for 2016* ✓ *In 2016, 95% applies* * **IRS will increase penalty each year.** **For 2015, it increased from $2000 to $2080.**	✓ *For 2015, no penalty* ✓ *A 50+ employer that avoids "A" penalty could be subject to the "B" penalty in 2016 if FT employee (part of 5% or 5 FT not offered MEC) gets PTC from Exchange* * **IRS will increase penalty each year.** **For 2015, it increased from $3000 to $3120.**

EITHER PENALTY MAY APPLY, NOT BOTH

"A" PENALTY 4980H (a)	B" PENALTY 4980H (b)
1. No offer of minimum essential coverage (MEC) 2. Trigger: FT employee gets Premium Tax Credit (PTC) from Exchange 3. $2080* x all FT employees 30 FT 2015: minus first 80 FT employees 2016: minus first 30 FT employees	1. Coverage is not affordable or does not provide minimum value 2. Trigger: FT employee gets Premium Tax Credit (PTC) from Exchange 3. $3120* x each FT employee who gets PTC from Exchange; never higher than employer would have received for "A" Penalty.

✓ Must offer to "all" FT employees
✓ Regulators defined "all" as 95% (all but greater of 5% or 5 FT)
✓ For 2015, lowered requirement to 70%
✓ In 2016, 95% applies
* IRS will increase this penalty each year.
  For 2015, it increased from $2000 to $2080.

EITHER PENALTY MAY APPLY BUT NOT BOTH

What do they mean by coverage being "affordable"?

To be considered affordable a job-based health plan can't cost more than 9.5% of employee's household income after employer contributions. However, most employers will use employee only income since they won't know household income for sure. If an employer offers multiple plans with at least the required minimum value, affordability is based on the lowest cost plan offered regardless of the plan the employee chooses. Be sure to take minimum wage increases into account when doing calculations to determine the affordability of your group coverage.

How much coverage do I have to offer?

A Health Plan meets minimum value if the plan's share of the total average costs of covered services is at least 60%. In other words, it must meet the basic requirements of a plan sold on the health insurance marketplace. Employers cannot discriminate in the way they offer health plans. For example, highly compensated employees cannot be offered options in a health plan that are not offered to all employees. Beginning in 2014, all individual and small group health plans must designate their actual value (percent of cost paid by the plan for covered benefits in-network) by metal tier. In 2016 these metal tier requirements also will apply to employers with 51 to 100 employees.

Bronze	Plan pays 60% of the costs for covered benefits in-network
Silver	Plan pays 70% of the costs for covered benefits in-network
Gold	Plan pays 80% of the costs for covered benefits in-network
Platinum	Plan pays 90% of the costs for covered benefits in-network

Will I get tax breaks for insuring my employees?

Small Businesses can apply for tax breaks of up to 50% (35% for non-profits) of their contribution to employees premiums if they have fewer than 25 full-time employees. To qualify, businesses must pay for at least 50% of their employees premiums and their workers average annual wages can't be more than $50,000 a year. To qualify for tax credits, insurance must be purchased on the Affordable Insurance Exchange for at least two years. Small business employers with over 25 full time employees will not have access to the same tax breaks as those small businesses with under 25 employees. Tax credits are available for small businesses on a sliding scale depending on the number of employees and average annual wages.

What do I need to tell my employees about health care?

If your company is covered by the Fair Labor Standards Act, it should provide a written notice to its employees about the Health Insurance Marketplace but there is no fine or penalty under the law for failing to provide the notice. The Department of Labor has model notices that employers can use to comply with the regulation. First class mail is the preferred way for notification. However, electronic mail is acceptable if it complies with the DOL electronic safe harbor elements. The ACA requires individual and group health plans to provide a uniform Summary of Benefits & Coverage (SBC) to all applicants and enrollees. Health insurance carriers offer SBCs on their websites in all required languages. Employees must be notified of modifications to the existing health plan at least 60 days prior to the effective date of the modification.

When do I need to provide health coverage to a new employee?

California AB 1083 set a 60-day waiting period from the date of hire to when coverage must be provided to an employee; rather than matching the federal requirement of a 90-day maximum. Employers can delay eligibility for up to an additional month to allow for a bona-fide orientation period during which the employee goes through training, and the employer and employee evaluate whether the new job is a good fit. Employers may have an eligibility requirement specifying the completion of a number of cumulative hours-of-service as long as the requirement does not exceed 1,200 hours and the waiting period begins as soon as the employee fulfils the requirement.

I own several small businesses each with fewer than 50 full time equivalent employees. How does the ACA affect me?

Good question. And be careful with this one! Two or more companies that have a common owner are combined for the purpose of calculating group size. This is referred to as a "Controlled Group" or by the IRS as an "Aggregated Group". The combined FTE calculation will render mandated responsibility or not on each individual organization regardless of the individual organization's group size. The types of Controlled Groups are:

- Brother-Sister
- Parent Subsidiary
- Combination

Brother-Sister: A group of two or more business in which 5 or fewer common owners own a "controlling interest" of the group and have "effective control" of the businesses.

- **"controlling interest"** – 80% or more of the stock of each corporation (but only if the   common owner owns stock in each corporation)

- **"effective control"** – More than 50% of the stock of each corporation counting the least of each owner's share.

Example: Step 1 Is total ownership equal to 80% or greater?

	Owner A	Owner B	Owner C	Total
~~XCorp~~	~~20%~~	~~30%~~	~~25%~~	~~75%~~
Y Corp	40%	10%	45%	95%
Z Corp	20%	40%	25%	85%

Step 2, Effective Control – Add the smallest interest each individual owns in each overlapping business. If that combined interest is greater than 50%, then a brother-sister Controlled Group exists

	Owner A	Owner B	Owner C	Total
~~XCorp~~	~~20%~~	~~30%~~	~~25%~~	~~75%~~
Y Corp	40%	**10%**	45%	95%
Z Corp	**20%**	40%	**25%**	85%

Parent-Subsidiary: One business owns a controlling interest (80% or more) in at least one other business. Example:

- Corporation A owns
- 90% of B Corp
- 85% of C Corp
- 65% of D Corp

Corp A would be a common parent of B and C and thus its employees would be added together to determining large employer status under the ACA.

Combination: Each business is a member of either a parent-subsidiary or brother-sister group AND at least one corporation is the common parent of a parent-subsidiary and is ALSO a member of a brother-sister group.

Example:

A owns
80% of Y Partnership and
90% of Z Corp

Y Partnership owns 85% of T Corp

Y Partnership, Z Corp and T Corp are members of the same controlled group under common control because all three are members of a parent-subsidiary or a brother-sister group and Y Partnership is the common parent of T Corp and a member of the Y Partnership – Z Corp brother-sister group.

What is transitional relief?

The ACA has been law for more than 5 years, however with legislation this complex there were, understandably, many kinks to work out. As we approach the first year where reporting requirements and penalties are being enforced, there are still many forms of relief available to employers to give them time to adjust their accounting and processes to comply with the ACA. The main types of transitional relief available are:

- Employers with between 50-99 FTEs for 2015 are not subject to the requirement to offer qualifying coverage to full time employees but must still meet the IRS reporting requirements for 2015.
- For 2015 employers who must offer qualifying coverage to full time employees must offer that

coverage to at least 70% of full time employees. In 2016 this increases to 95%.

There are six more forms of transitional relief available for 2015. Please check the IRS website for more information that you may find useful.

What is a "grandfathered" health insurance plan? What is a "grandmothered" plan and how are they different?

A grandfathered health insurance plan is one that existed prior to the signing of the ACA law, March 23, 2010, that provides less coverage than the ACA requires. If you have a grandfathered plan and like it, you can keep it indefinitely as long as it does not substantially cut benefits or increase costs to consumers. A grandfathered plan does not have to comply with the following ACA requirements:

- Cover preventive care for free
- Guarantee your right to appeal a coverage decision
- Protect your choice of doctors and access to emergency care
- Be held accountable through Rate Review for excessive premium increases

In addition to the above, grandfathered *individual* health insurance plans (the kind you buy yourself, not the kind you get from an employer) *don't* have to:

- End yearly limits on coverage
- Cover you if you have a pre-existing health condition

Grandmothered plans are a form of transitional relief. They can be in effect after March 23, 2010 and still provide less than the minimum required benefit but are expected to be phased out in the coming years. Each state can individually choose whether or not grandmothered health plans can continue to be renewed through, at this point, September of 2017 when federal law will require they be replaced with ACA compliant plans.

What are the reporting requirements under the ACA?

Under IRS code sections 6055 and 6056, starting in fiscal year 2015 the IRS requires employers with 50 or more employees to complete forms 1095-C and 1094-C. Those employers must complete the forms even if they have less than 100 employees and are operating under transitional relief for 2015. Form 1095-C must be completed for all full time employees and provided to each of them no later than Jan 31st of the year following the calendar year, so Jan 31st, 2016 for the year 2015. Form 1094-C and copies of 1095-C must be filed with the IRS by the employer no later than Feb 28th of the year following the calendar year (March 31 if filing electronically), so Feb 28th, 2016 for the year 2015 (March 31st, 2016 if filing electronically).

It is no surprise that completing these forms is a fairly complex process. Check the IRS website for copies of the forms and instructions. Also follow up with your tax preparer, payroll company, and/or accountant to make sure all are on the same page. The information that will need to be collected monthly is:

- Your total number of full time and full time equivalent employees
- Whether or not you offered a qualifying health plan to full time employees
  (if using transitional relief i.e.: for 2015 you had 50-99 FTEs, this must be indicated as well)
- Whether or not you are a member of an aggregated group (Controlled Group) and information about the other group members if you are
- For each employee offered coverage the amount of the employee's share of the lowest cost monthly premium you are offering

CHAPTER 3

Worker's Comp or Retaliation? Control Claims and Lower Your Premium!

The vast majority of your employees are honest, dependable people. They're an asset to your business. Once in a while, temptation can be too much, though. I had a client whose bookkeeper convinced him to let her make deposits and reconcile the bank accounts. Not good! Sure enough over a period of time certain deposits found their way into the bookkeepers pocket. She also issued payroll checks to former employees, but endorsed them to herself and cashed them. This all went on for 3 years and $500,000. Another client allowed managers to delete transactions within their point of sale system. Not void, but totally delete. This was supposed to save time and paperwork. It was not supposed to give the manager the opportunity to walk away with $50,000, but that's what happened. Don't let this happen to you.

When you open your doors it comes with a lot of risk. You could have a fire, a theft, burst pipes, a customer could slip and fall, get food poisoning, break a tooth. It is vital to know what these risks are and how to make sure you're covered properly. This chapter will explain some information about property and liability coverage, what to do if you have a claim, and how to protect yourself so you can get on with what you're good at - the day to day activities of running a restaurant.

The Questions Clients Mostly Ask

1. What is tenant improvements and betterments coverage and how much coverage do I need?

Tenant improvements are defined as property owned and installed by the tenant that is affixed to the building. Counters, light fixtures, major kitchen equipment, shelving, and many decorative elements are examples of tenant improvements. In general, tenant improvements become part of the building and cannot be removed once the tenant vacates the building. The amount of coverage for tenant improvements and betterments should be equal to 100% of the replacement value.

2. What is business personal property and what does it cover? How much coverage do I need?

Business personal property is everything the business owns that is not a tenant improvement or real property. Utensils, dishware, flatware, small appliances, the POS system, and inventory are examples of business personal property. The amount of coverage for business personal property should be equal to 100% of the replacement value.

3. What is the difference between tenant improvements and business personal property?

Tenant improvements are defined as property owned and installed by the tenant that is affixed to the building. Counters, light fixtures, major kitchen equipment, shelving, and many decorative elements are examples of tenant improvements. In general, tenant improvements become part of the building and cannot be removed once the tenant vacates the building.

Business personal property is everything the business owns that is not a tenant improvement or real property. Utensils, dishware, flatware, small appliances, the POS system, and inventory are examples of business personal property.

4. How much liability insurance do I need?

The amount of a liability claim is one of the biggest unknown factors a business can face. The rule of thumb is to have as much liability coverage as you can afford. A business can be devastated by a large judgment in a lawsuit not to mention the cost of defending lengthy litigation. Once your insurance limits have run out or the limits of the policy have been offered and declined, the business owner is on their own to cover any additional or continuing costs out of pocket.

Your liability limits should be at least $1,000,000. If you can afford an umbrella, it is strongly advised you purchase the largest limit you can. Umbrella policies are generally quite inexpensive. Many lease agreements are requiring high limits of liability and umbrella policies.

5. How do I insure special events or catering?

Make sure your broker is aware of the fact that you offer catering and whether it is on and/or off your premises. Your property/liability policy will generally cover catering events on your premises automatically but catering off premises might require additional coverage. He/she will be able to make sure you have what you need including:

- Coverage for any vehicles owned by or rented to you for off premises catering

- Coverage for liability arising from your employees use of their own vehicles for delivery or catering

- Liquor liability if you will be serving liquor at the event

- Adequate coverage for your business property that is taken off premises for catering

- Adequate coverage for liability claims from food poisoning, chipped tooth claims, spills, and burns, etc.

6. How can I reduce claims?

It is critical to have a routine inspection process in place for your business. It should include daily, weekly, and monthly inspections. Some items to look for are:

- If you have steps are they clear and visible? Is there a "watch your step" sign?

- Do you have a procedure to clean up spills as quickly as possible to prevent slip and fall claims?

- Make sure kitchen procedures are in place to prevent spoilage of perishable items and foreign objects in food.

- Repair any broken property as soon as possible. Make sure your landlord is aware of and repairs any property that is his/her responsibility.

- Make sure your fire suppression system is serviced at least every six months and flues, hoods and ducts are cleaned quarterly. Have a contract with a company that will do this regularly as well as recharging hand-held fire extinguishers

- Make sure you have an adequate number of extinguishers and they are of the right type

It is also imperative to have regularly scheduled meetings and training for your staff to reinforce safety issues. These meetings should be held at least quarterly.

See if your carrier offers loss control services. If they do, make sure you take advantage of them. Many insurance companies do routine safety inspections and make recommendations. Make sure to comply with these as they are designed specifically to help you reduce claims.

7. How should I handle claims?

An incident report should be completed in the event of any customer injury or illness and sent to your broker to forward to the insurance carrier. NEVER discuss who is liable or offer an immediate settlement to someone who has been injured or becomes ill at your restaurant. Doing so can jeopardize your defense and your coverage. Immediately forward any legal papers received to your broker and/or your claims adjuster.

In the event of damage to your property, it is your responsibility to secure the property from further damage when possible. Contact a disaster repair company who can help and advise you if damage occurs outside of normal business hours. Document the damage and take photos whenever practical. Contact your broker as soon as you can to describe what has been damaged, how the damage occurred, and when it occurred. Forward any repair bills and estimates including bills for anything you did to protect property to your broker. If you have to close your business due to the damage you will need to provide current and historic financial data to the adjuster in order to have the business income portion of the claim settled. It is a good idea to start gathering that information right away. Sales and expense journals, and P&L statements are a good start. Remember you will need to provide these for the last few months before the claim and probably also for the same period the prior year.

8. Do I need umbrella coverage? How much coverage do I need?

We highly recommend umbrella policies. Many lease agreements now require this coverage. An umbrella policy provides an additional layer of liability protection should you be named in a large lawsuit. Amounts awarded in legal judgments are on the rise, as are class action suits. The judgment amount is ultimately determined by a judge and jury when a case goes to trial. <u>Once your insurance limits have run out or the limits of the policy have been offered and declined, the business owner is on their own to cover any additional or continuing costs out of pocket.</u> An umbrella policy will provide valuable additional legal defense costs as well as costs of judgments in excess of your underlying liability limits.

9. I have no claims so why are my insurance rates getting higher?

There are many factors the affect the cost of an insurance policy. The largest, of course, is the cost of claims. When you pay your insurance premium your money goes into a pool along with the premiums of all other businesses insured by the same company. When you or another insured business have a claim the money to pay that claim is taken from that pool. If an insurance company experiences higher claims for all restaurants they insure as a group, then each individual restaurant in that group would be asked to pay a little more so that there is always enough money in the pool to pay all the claims. The best way to reduce the amount of money needed to pay claims is for each individual restaurant owner to take aggressive action to reduce the likelihood that they will have a claim.

10. If I use my personal car for business use or my employee uses their own personal vehicle is it covered under my policy?

It depends on the type of business use. If a car is used to run errands, go to the bank, call on clients or vendors, etc., then generally the answer is yes. You or your employee's personal auto policy will protect you or the employee and if you have non-owned auto coverage on your business policy, then the business is protected as well.

If you use your car or your employees use their own cars for delivery or transportation of customers a special policy is needed to cover that type of use. Ask your broker about specialized non-owned auto coverage for delivery and/or specialized auto coverage for livery (transporting customers).

11. Does my personal umbrella cover me in my business and will my business umbrella cover me for personal claims?

No. Personal liability policies, including umbrellas, cover your personal activities only. You need a commercial umbrella policy for your business and vice-versa.

The Questions Clients Should be Asking

1. What is difference between admitted and non-admitted companies?

An admitted carrier files certain documents and rates with the State Department of Insurance and is protected by a state's guarantee fund should the company become insolvent while you have a pending claim. A non-admitted carrier is not.

2. How do I reduce or eliminate employee dishonesty, theft, embezzlement?

First and foremost, make sure every employee knows how the company defines employee theft and the repercussions if someone is caught stealing. It is imperative to install and use available technology to monitor inventory and cash handling and watch for suspicious patterns, an unusual number of voided transactions, etc. If you can, use video monitoring. This can also be useful as a training tool as you can use the video to review employee performance.

3. If I find an employee that has embezzled from me, what should I do?

Make sure you have adequate proof before confronting an employee about theft or embezzlement. This can be bank records, POS system receipts, inventory control records, etc. Also consult with legal counsel and have an employment practice liability policy in place prior to terminating an employee. Your employee handbook should state that you reserve the right to inspect lockers and break room areas at any time and employees should sign off that they have read and understand the handbook. You should notify your broker right away so that a claim can be started under your employee dishonesty coverage.

4. What insurance coverage protects me against employee dishonesty, stealing, or embezzlement?

Employee dishonesty coverage. Without this you are only protected against theft by someone other than an employee.

5. Can I get coverage for assault and battery and is that an important coverage?

Assault and battery refers to a situation where a customer claims they were assaulted by your employee or contractor (bouncer, doorman, server, security, etc.), or another customer. The general liability policy covers this type of claim, HOWEVER sometimes insurance companies will remove this coverage by endorsement. This is usually known as assault and battery exclusion. Insurance companies apply this exclusion if they feel you are more likely to have such incidents; you are a night club, are open past midnight, have a large percentage of liquor sales, etc. If you see this on your policy, notify your broker so they can discuss with you your options.

6. Are off premises power failure, food spoilage, and loss of business covered in my policy?

A power failure that occurs off premises can result in the closing of your business for a day or longer and result in the loss of customer business during that time as well as food spoilage. Some companies apply a waiting period to this coverage. For example, if you have a 24 hour waiting period on your policy for off premises power failure, it means the insurance company will not pay for lost income that happens in the first 24 hours immediately after the failure. This is like a deductible. You must have specific endorsements attached to your policy to be covered for off premises power failure. Your broker can discuss with you your available coverage options.

Many companies offer specific coverage endorsements for food contamination. Your liability policy will pay for food poisoning illness to customers, but not lost income and crisis management costs if you have to close due to a more widespread incident of contamination. Make sure you discuss this potential coverage gap with your broker and how to cover it.

7. Is equipment failure covered in my insurance policy?

Equipment breakdown used to be known as "boiler and machinery" coverage. It now covers a great deal more than pressurized equipment and machines. Equipment breakdown provides coverage for internal sources of damage to your machinery and equipment, such as your POS system, and refrigeration system. Internal sources of damage include power surges, faulty wiring, short circuit, and mechanical failure. Internal sources of damage are not covered by the standard policy.

8. How do I cover my credit card processing system if it is hacked?

In today's world, cybercrime is a huge and growing problem. Business owners are often responsible for the protection of their customer's personal information. No matter how secure yours is, though, every system is vulnerable to hackers. A cyber liability policy or endorsement will protect you against the enormous expenses that can be incurred if your customer's personal information is obtained and used for fraudulent purposes. Ask your broker for more information and refer to the cybercrime section of this book.

9. Do I need to insure independent contractors that work for me like doormen, ID checkers and bouncers?

If you hire doormen, ID checkers, bouncers or anyone else as employees then they are covered under your policy as any other employee would be. Many restaurants, though, choose to use independent contractors for these types of positions. It is best to insist they have their own coverage in place as independent business people and that you be named as additional insured on their policy. This is also true of valets. If you contract directly with a valet company, make sure they are insured and you are named on their policy. Ask the independent contractor you hire for proof in the form of a certificate of insurance.

10. What is the best way to insure drivers and delivery people?

If your restaurant offers delivery you need specialized coverage for your liability. If your drivers use their own vehicles to deliver, you need non-owned auto coverage specifically for delivery. If your business owns the vehicles used for delivery, you need business auto insurance. Your general liability policy does not cover delivery. If you start offering this service to your customers you need to contact your broker right away to make sure you have the coverage you need.

11. What insurance coverage is needed when I sign a lease and/or open my restaurant?

Your lease agreement will spell out exactly what the insurance requirements are. Have your broker review this section of the lease to make sure you are in compliance. You'll also need coverage for your business property and tenant improvements. If you are remodeling or doing ground up construction prior to opening, you'll need special insurance for the period of construction. If you are using a contractor, make sure they have insurance and have named your business as additional insured. If you have hired employees, you'll need worker's comp coverage in place. In California, the State Board of Equalization will require a sales tax bond that guarantees your tax payment if you default. If you are considering opening a new restaurant, make sure your broker is informed and involved early in the process.

12. What determines if I need to Insure my building if I am in a freestanding location?

If you own the building then you will need to have building coverage. You will also need to have it if your lease agreement requires you to insure the building. Your broker can review your lease and advise if you need this.

13. What documentation is required to purchase property and liability coverage?

If you have prior ownership experience, your broker will need documentation of your claims history. This documentation is known as "loss runs." Usually three or four years worth of loss runs are needed depending on the type of coverage, and if you've had a number of claims in the past. Many insurance companies are also requiring financial information. They may attempt to check credit history as this is a good indicator of the possibility of future claims. If you are new to ownership, insurance companies will ask you to provide details of your prior restaurant experience. If you have managed restaurants in the past, they will want to know when and where. Providing copies of your current declarations pages to your broker, if you have current insurance, can be very helpful in making sure you have all the coverage you need at the proper limits.

Business Insurance Checklist:

___ Property policy has been reviewed and limits are equal to 100% of replacement value of all property and equipment.

___ Liability limits have been reviewed. They are at least $1,000,000 and higher if available and not cost prohibitive.

___ An umbrella policy is in place if available and not cost prohibitive.

___ Catering and delivery activities, if applicable, have been discussed with my insurance agent and proper coverage is place for such things as any driving exposure.

___ My policy includes coverage for off premises power failure, utility services and food spoilage.

___ My policy includes coverage for assault and battery.

___ My insurance agent has reviewed my lease to make sure additional insureds are included properly and the policy contains all coverage required by my landlord.

___ Routine physical inspections of the restaurant are regularly conducted and a form is used to note anything that needs to be addressed/repaired.

___ Safety meetings are regularly held with all staff to emphasize the importance of maintaining public areas for all guests and immediately addressing any potential hazards.

___ An incident report form is available to document any accidents involving a guest and the completed form is immediately forwarded to my insurance agent.

___ All staff have been instructed about what to do in case of a guest accident and have been told never to discuss such incidents with anyone other than my insurance agent, company claims adjuster and/or company assigned attorney.

CHAPTER 4

Understanding Business Insurance Liability and Managing Your Risk?

"Common sense" is actually very uncommon. So, when in doubt please explain it, write it, teach it, train it, post it, demonstrate it, and repeat. You would never think you have to mention "please do not stand on top of the stove and straddle the deep fat fryer while it is on and trying to clean the hood." Really not a smart idea. What can happen is that you lose your balance and step in the fryer causing a permanent disability, and sue the restaurant owner and get awarded over $450,000.00 in settlement. The restaurant owner's California worker's compensation rating experience mod, and the impact on his insurance rates, took the restaurant out of business permanently. This claim was over ten years ago. In today's standard, it would be way over a million dollar settlement. If it can happen to him, it can happen to you.

Remember when you were young, and your parents taught you how to cross the street safely? You were told never to jaywalk. We had a client whose employee, tragically, didn't get that lesson. He was on a paid break, ran across the street to buy a lottery ticket, and was hit by a car and fatally injured. Since he was on the clock, it was work comp. To the tune of $400,000. With that claim and the increased ex-mod, the employer's premium more than doubled. If it can happen to him, it can happen to you.

A recent national survey found that 90% of people know what worker's compensation is. Of that group, roughly half knew someone who had filed a worker's compensation claim. Of those who knew a claimant, nearly 25% said they believed the claim was fraudulent!

Worker's compensation Insurance is required by law if you have even one employee. The premium for this coverage can be a significant part of a business owner's budget. That is why it is so important to make sure you are getting the best available rates. In this chapter, we will explain how worker's comp insurance works, and how to control your costs.

The Questions Clients Mostly Ask

1. What determines my worker's compensation rates and premium?

Your worker's compensation premium is based primarily on your annual payroll. Your claims history also has an impact on your premium, as does the type of business, the classification of your employees by job type, your experience modification factor, and the discounts the insurance company is willing to offer. Workers Compensation insurance premium rates are not regulated by the state. While the Workers Compensation Insurance Rating Bureau-the licensed statistical agent for the state insurance commissioner issues recommended rates and carriers must file their rates with California Department of Insurance, rates can vary from carrier to carrier.

2. Why has my worker's compensation rate increased when I have had no or minimal claims?

Your own claims are only one factor in determining worker's compensation rates. When you pay your insurance premium, your money goes into a pool along with the premiums of all other businesses insured by the same company. When you or another insured business have a claim, the money to pay that claim is taken from that pool. If an insurance company experiences higher claims for all restaurants they insure as a group, then each individual restaurant in that group would be asked to pay a little more so that there is always enough money in the pool to pay all the claims. The best way to reduce the amount of money needed to pay claims is for each individual restaurant owner to take aggressive action to reduce the likelihood that they will have a claim.

3. What is an ex-mod and how does it impact my worker's comp rates?

Your experience modification can result in a higher or a lower premium. Its purpose is to estimate the likelihood of claims for your particular business compared to the average expected claims for all business of the same type. Your prior claims history, payroll, and premium are all used to calculate your experience modifier (ex-mod). If your ex-mod is 1.00, it means your premium is neither discounted nor surcharged. If it is 1.25, it means your premium will be surcharged 25%. If it is .85, it means your premium will be discounted 15%. Typically you will receive an Experience Modification Rating Sheet each year prior to your policy renewal date.

4. Do I pay a different worker's comp rate if I am new in business as opposed to having prior experience?

Maybe. If you have prior experience and low claims, you may be able to get coverage with a carrier with more preferred rates. On the other hand, if you have prior experience, it may be reflected in your ex-mod which can result in either higher or lower rates.

5. Am I legally required to implement a safety program or IIPP (Injury Illness Prevention Program)?

It depends on the state. In California, employers are required to have an effective IIPP. Many insurance companies are also now requiring proof that a program is in place. Your broker can help you develop an IIPP if you don't already have one. An IIPP can be a very effective tool to reduce worker compensation claims and, in turn, lower your premium. The 8 required injury and Illness Prevention Program elements are:

1. Responsibility
2. Compliance
3. Communication
4. Hazard Assessment
5. Accident/Exposure Investigation
6. Hazard Correction
7. Training and Instruction
8. Recordkeeping

To be effective your IIPP must:

- Fully involve all employees, supervisors, and management
- Identify the specific workplace hazards employees are exposed to
- Correct identified hazards in an appropriate and timely Manner
- Provide effective training

6. Who is exempt for worker's compensation? Do I need to insure family members?

Owners of the business are usually exempt. This means individuals if a sole prop., partners if a partnership, and corporate officers if they are shareholders. Family members are not exempt and need to be insured unless they fall into one of these categories.

7. Who is covered by a worker's comp policy?

Your employees are covered by Worker's Comp as required by law. It is important to note that if you hire as independent contractors; doormen, ID checkers, bouncers, etc. they are normally not covered by Worker's Comp. It is extremely important to check with your CPA to ensure they are truly independent contractors, though, or if they must be covered.

8. Is worker's compensation auditable?

Yes. All worker's compensation policies are subject to audit. The audit can be done by mail for a very small business or done in person. The auditor will ask for documentation of your payroll records, and job descriptions for all employees to make sure they are properly classified. He/she will also ask for information as to ownership of the business to confirm who should be exempt. Contact your broker if you have questions or concerns about your audit results. Failure to pay audit premium due or failure to comply with an audit can result in policy cancellation. It is important to pay the audit bill even if the audit is in dispute. If the dispute ends up in your favor, the payment you made plus any over-payments that result will be returned. This is a much better alternative than being without coverage.

9. How do I reduce the worker's compensation premium for my business?

An effective injury and illness prevention program is a great start. Having an employee bulletin board in place where safe lifting tips and safe cutting tips are posted is also effective. Frequent and regular safety meetings are also an important way to reduce claims and lower your insurance costs. Continual monitoring of your employees is a very good way to recognize safety issues and correct them before they turn into claims. Some employers use an incentive program to reward employees for always applying safe practices in the workplace.

10. Will my insurance company fight a fraud claim? Do insurance companies pay suspected fraud claims?

Insurance companies actively investigate and report fraud and abuse of the worker's compensation system. That being said, companies are subject to state laws and regulations, and fraud may be hard to define or prove. If you suspect fraud, report it to the worker's compensation insurance company for further action.

11. Can I terminate an employee that has filed a worker's comp claim?

In general, no. You should always check with a knowledgeable Worker's Comp attorney before taking such an action. In June 2014, the Worker's Compensation Research Institute identified several new predictors of worker outcomes. They found trust in the workplace to be one of the more important predictors that has never been examined before. To calculate the level of trust or mistrust in the work environment, interviewers asked workers if they were concerned about being fired as a result of the injury. Here are some of the key findings:

- Workers who were strongly concerned about being fired after the injury experienced poorer return-to-work outcomes than workers without those concerns.

- One in five workers who were concerned about being fired reported that they were not working at the time of the interview. Among workers who were not concerned about being fired, only one in 10 workers was not working at the time of the interview.

- Concerns about being fired were associated with an average four-week increase in the duration of disability.

As you can see from the above, creating an environment where workers are not worried about being fired for an injury can even lower your claim amounts and your premiums!

12. What are worker's compensation employee classifications, and how are they determined?

Employee classifications are determined by the WCIRB

(Worker's Compensation Insurance Rating Bureau), an independent non-profit association that provides statistical information to insurance companies. A classification attempts to group employees together who have the same general duties and risk of injury during their regular work day. Classifications exist so that employers do not pay the same rate for a low-risk employee (general office work) as they do a higher risk (demolition expert).

13. How long can claims impact my worker's compensation rates?

There are two answers. An insurance company can ask to see 3-5 years or more prior claims history to determine your rate, and if any discounts may be available. Usually not more than 5, though. Your ex-mod goes back five years into your claims history.

The Questions Clients Should be Asking

1. What are some ways I can prevent or reduce worker's comp claims?

- 5% of claims can usually be prevented. See if your insurance carrier offers online reports, safety tips, and/or video libraries and take advantage of these resources if they do.

- Make sure you have safety programs in place and hold regularly scheduled meetings with staff to reinforce your policies and procedures.

- Create incentive programs. One of our clients greatly reduced worker's comp claims by offering lottery tickets to all staff for every month there were no claims.

- Consult with legal counsel who are experts in labor or worker's compensation issues.

- Consider using an independent expert to consult with you on the best practices for your business. Your broker may be one or may, at least, know who to refer you to.

2. How can I close up worker's comp claims and lower reserves?

Open claims and high reserves can have an effect on your ex-mod. You should review your claims history annually/semi-annually with the help of your broker and determine if any outstanding claims can be closed or reserves lowered. Don't forget about your current year's claims. These usually present the greatest opportunity for cost reductions. Remember this year's claims will affect your ex-mod next year. Reserves are amounts insurance companies set aside to pay the cost of workers' compensation claims. The Sarbanes-Oxley Act of 2002 and other regulations require insurance companies to accurately document their liabilities. Workers compensation claims are considered an owed obligation, a legal liability for the insurance company. Some brokers use monitoring companies that will help to lower reserves and close claims. See if your broker does as this can be a great way to lower your ex-mod, and subsequently, your work comp premiums. The critical date is unit stat filing time which occurs six months after the effective date of your policy. It is important that any claims that can be closed out or reserves lowered are done so before the information is sent in to the Workers Compensation Insurance Rating Bureau.

Reserves consist of Medical, Indemnity and Expense:

Medical:

- To establish the amount of the medial reserve, the adjuster will analyze the medical reports to provide an informed estimate of the cost in the following sub-categories:
- Physicals
- Specialist
- Diagnostic Testing
- Hospitals
- Physical Therapy/Occupational Therapy
- Pharmacy
- Transportation (to/from Medical Care)
- Attendant Care

Indemnity:

To establish the amount of the indemnity reserve, the adjuster will analyze the medical reports and discuss with the employer the modified duty options, to provide an informed estimate of the claim cost in the following sub categories:

- Temporary Total Disability
- Temporary Partial Disability
- Permanent Partial Disability
- Permanent Total Disability
- Vocational Rehabilitation
- Death Benefits
- Dependent Benefits

Expense:

The adjuster will consider all aspects of the claims to estimate the dollar amount of the sub-categories of the expense Reserve. (Note the expense amount does not go into the experience modification calculation).

- Defense Attorneys
- Court Costs
- Court Reporters
- Experts
- Surveillance
- State Filing Fees
- Peer Reviews
- Independent Medical Examinations
- Medical Reports
- Medical Management

3. How do insurance companies set reserve amounts?

The information needed to establish a precise reserve is normally not available at the time the claim is assigned to an adjuster. Often the necessary medical information to establish the reserve will not be forthcoming until weeks or even months into the claim. There are two primary approaches adjusters use to set the initial reserve early in the claim before medical information is available. The first is a combination of guessing and estimating based on what claims with similar injuries have cost in the past. The second is a statistical reserve where all claims have the same initial reserve amount based on the historical average cost of claims. Either method should be revisited once the necessary medical information has been obtained.

4. After a worker's comp injury, should I offer modified/light duty to my employee?

If you can offer modified/light duty work to an employee, it can be an effective way to lower worker's comp premiums by reducing disability claims costs. It can also increase productivity for your business by avoiding having to hire and train a new or temporary employee.

5. How do I combat fraudulent claims?

Sometimes people do take advantage of the worker's compensation system. Here are some notable examples:

"An actor collected more than $51,000 in disability benefits after being injured when a piece of ceiling fell on him while working as a dancer. The actor continued to accept disability payments even while advancing his career landing a high-profile role as one of Kia's dancing hamsters in their well-known car commercials. He also used alias names to work as a backup dancer for Madonna, Kelly Roland, and Chris Brown. He faces up to 10 years in prison for fraud."

"A former Los Angeles Unified School District police officer was arrested for worker's compensation fraud for exaggerating the extent of his injuries. The former officer allegedly sustained work-related injuries while patrolling campus on a bicycle when he ran over, slipped and fell on a "wayward cantaloupe". The man initially claimed injuries to his right knee, right foot, and right hand, but after obtaining legal counsel he added injuries to his back, hips, and both knees. He also denied any prior injuries to these additional body parts, however subpoenaed medical records indicated otherwise."

"A doctor in California was sentenced to five years of probation with 12 months of home confinement for defrauding the Federal Government and submitting fraudulent worker's compensation claims of over $170,000. His sentence would have been much more severe had it not been for the unique circumstances of his case. During his emotional plea to the judge, the 72-year-old doctor explained that he intentionally overbilled patients whose costs were covered by the government so he could afford to treat those who couldn't pay. His seemingly sincere remorse and concern for his patients played into the judge's relatively light sentence."

"If you're going to collect disability, it's probably best not to take on work as a masseur. A man, 53, in Torrance, California learned that the hard way when an investigation revealed that he was gainfully employed as a message therapist, despite receiving benefits for a debilitating shoulder injury. The man was supposedly injured while employed by the U.S. Postal Service, but failed to report his improvement of condition, or new career path, to the U.S. Department of Labor, the entity that handles worker's compensation for the U.S. Postal Service. The man faces one count of insurance fraud. Not to mention a royal pain in the neck."

If you suspect fraud on the part of an employee claiming worker's comp benefits, report your concerns to the insurance company handling the claim. DO NOT confront the employee or anyone else directly, and make sure you have documented facts to support your position. The information you provide at the onset is important since the claim can be denied within the first 90 days of being reported to you.

6. Do I pay worker's comp premiums based on gross or net payroll?

Worker's comp premiums are based on gross payroll less certain exclusions. You can exclude 1/3 of overtime paid at 1.5 times the regular rate and 1/2 overtime paid at 2 times the regular rate. You can also exclude tips and gratuities.

7. Are worker's comp rates fixed or negotiable?

Negotiable, and it is your broker's responsibility to aggressively negotiate on your behalf to get you the lowest rate possible. A larger broker is frequently in a better position to negotiate for additional credits.

8. How do I verify my audit?

Your broker can obtain detailed audit results from the insurance company. You should review them with your actual payroll reports. Make sure overtime and tips are properly excluded, employees are classified correctly, and exempt owners' payroll is not being included. If you find discrepancies, provide documentation for them to your broker, and tell him/her you with to contest the audit. In most cases, you must still pay the audit premium to keep your policy in force, but if the dispute is resolved in your favor, you'll get the audit payment back plus any overpayment you are due.

9. What is a worker's compensation unit status filing report and how does it affect my ex-mod?

A unit status filing report is sent by a worker's comp insurance company to the worker's compensation insurance rating bureau. It contains your claim and premium information for the past years, and is what the bureau will use to calculate your ex-mod.

10. What services are available to a business owner to assist with claims, reduce reserves, and verify unit status filing reports?

There are a number of companies that will assist with these things and help you lower your ex-mod whenever possible. Ask your broker if they have access to one of these companies. These services can go a long way toward lowering your worker's comp insurance costs.

Worker's Comp and Workplace Safety Checklist:

__ Accurate payroll records are kept and are available for worker's comp audits.

__Employees are properly classified based on their actual job duties.

__My worker's comp policy has been reviewed. Payroll and job classification estimates are accurate.

__My ex-mod has been reviewed, and my insurance agent contacted to see if a monitoring company is available to keep an eye on open claims and potentially lower the rate.

__I have a workplace safety program in place as required by law.

__All required state and federal labor postings are up in a conspicuous area as required by law.

__Regular staff meetings are held stressing workplace safety.

__An incentive program is in place to reward employees for no workplace accidents, if applicable.

__All necessary safety equipment is available and in good working condition. Employees are informed that use of such equipment is not optional.

__I have a modified/light duty return to work program in place, if possible.

__In case of an accident, the claims reporting telephone number is posted in a highly visible place such as on the employee bulletin board.

__Any claims packets and/or "what to do in case of a claim" information from my insurance carrier has been reviewed.

A

A.M. BEST COMPANY - Founded in 1899, A.M. Best Company is a full-service credit rating organization dedicated to serving the insurance industry. Policyholders refer to Best's ratings and analysis as a means of assessing the financial strength and creditworthiness of risk-bearing entities and investment vehicles.

ACCIDENT YEAR - The year in which a particular injury (or injuries) occurred.

ACCIDENT YEAR EXPERIENCE – Matching Accident Year Losses with Accident Year Premium. Accident Year Experience changes as losses develop and premium finalizes.

ACCIDENT YEAR LOSSES - The losses that occurred during an accident year. Accident Year Losses, per year, change as claims develop. The ultimate Accident Year Losses are known once all claims that accident year are settled.

ACCIDENT YEAR PREMIUM - The combined premium that is attributed to the accident year. Accident Year Premium, per year, changes as premium adjusts in subsequent years. The ultimate Accident Year Premium is known once all premium adjustments are finalized. Accident Year premium includes the pro rata portion of premium activity for the Accident Year.

ACTUARY - An individual that projects a liability value using mathematical, accounting and statistical analysis of past loss data.

ADJUDICATION - resolving a controversy between parties by litigating the legal and/or factual issues. The court hearing usually pronounces a judgment based on the presented evidence.

ADJUSTER - Individual who settles a claim filed by an insured. The adjuster evaluates the claim and determines the proceeds that may be payable for the claim.

ADJUSTMENT - The process of settling a claim. The settlement process includes evaluating the cause and amount of a loss, and determining the coverage and payment of any proceeds required under the insurance policy.

ADL - Activities of Daily Living.

ADMITTED ASSETS - The assets that are permitted by state insurance to determine the financial condition of an insurance company.

ADJUSTING AND OTHER EXPENSES (A&O) - The loss adjustment expenses not related to the **defense**, litigation or cost containment of a claim. This includes the cost of adjusters and the cost of inspectors appraisers fraud inspectors while working in the capacity of an adjuster.

AGGREGATE LIMIT - The maximum amount the insurer will pay for all claims covered by a policy during that policy period.

ANNIVERSARY RATING DATE (ARD) – The date that determines the effective rates on a policy. It is usually the effective date of the policy (unless the rating board establishes a different date).

ANNUAL STATEMENT - The annual report an insurance company is required to file with the state insurance department in each state in which they do business. The report provides information that the insurance company has adequate reserves, and that the assets are available to meet all benefit payments for which they are liable.

ASSIGNED RISK - A policyholder that is unable to obtain voluntary insurance coverage and is assigned to the carrier of last resort, or to a pool of participating insurers.

ASSUME - The acceptance by a reinsurer (assuming company), of part or all of the written insurance transferred to it by the primary insurer or another reinsurer.

ASSUMING COMPANY - The reinsurance company that accepts risk from a primary insurer or another reinsurer.

B

BASIC PREMIUM - Basic Premium is a percentage of the standard premium used in calculating the premium of a retrospectively rated policy. The portion of the retrospective premium that is loaded to reflect a policy's expected overhead cost and profit.

BENEFITS - Monetary payments (and other services provided) by insurers to the insured party under the terms of an insurance policy.

BULK RESERVES - An additional amount added to reserves to account for claim development not included in the case reserves. Bulk Reserves cannot be attributed to individual claims, but are an adjustment related to all outstanding claims.

C

CALENDAR YEAR EXPERIENCE - Matching Calendar Year Losses with Calendar Year Premiums.

CALENDAR YEAR LOSSES - The combined losses that occurred during a calendar year Calendar Year Losses include claim activity the current year claims and additional claim activity for prior year claims that occurred during a given calendar year.

CALENDAR YEAR PREMIUM - The combined premium that transpired during a calendar year. Calendar Year Premium includes premium activity for the current calendar year only, regardless of the policy period.

CANCELLATION - Termination of an insurance policy before its expiration date. This can be done by either the insurance company or the policyholder.

CARRIER OF LAST RESORT - The insurance company designated to accept a policyholder that has been refused coverage by all other insurance companies. The Carrier of Last Resort is usually a state fund.

CEDE - The act of transferring all or part of the insurance written by an insurer (ceding company), to reduce the possible liability of the insurer.

CEDING COMPANY - The insurance company that transfers risk to a reinsurer.

CERTIFICATE OF INSURANCE - The document issued by the insurance company that provides evidence of a policyholder's insurance coverage.

CLAIM - A request made by or on behalf of a claimant to an insurance company for payment of a loss covered by an insurance policy.

CLAIMANT - An individual who submits a claim to an insurance company for an incurred loss.

CLAIMS OUTSTANDING (OR CLAIMS PENDING) - The total number of open claims a policyholder has at any given time.

CLAIMS RESERVES - The reserves attributed to an individual outstanding claim. Claims Reserves are equal to total incurred less net payments (gross payments less subrogation).

CLAIMS SEVERITY - Average cost per claim. Severity can be based on accident year or policy year, for an individual, group or all policies.

CLASS CODES - A numerical index by type of business operations used in grouping similar type of risks for rating purposes. Class Codes are developed so that businesses with similar characteristics are charged the same rate.

COLLECTED PREMIUM - The amount of premium that has been received as payment for an insurance policy.

COMBINED RATIO - The sum of the loss ratio and expense ratio. Combined Ratio shows if an insurance company is making a profit on the business it is writing, without taking into account the investment returns on the premium received.

COVERAGE A - Workers' compensation policy under which the insurance company promises to pay all compensation and benefits required of an insured employer under the workers' compensation act of the state (or states) listed on the policy.

COVERAGE B - Workers' compensation policy for situations in which an employee not covered under workers' compensation law could sue for injuries suffered under common law liability.

D

DEATH BENEFITS - Indemnity benefits paid to the eligible survivor of a worker whose injuries resulted in death. The benefits are usually paid until the surviving spouse remarries, or is determined to no longer be dependent on the benefits. After the remarriage of the spouse, or in the absence of a surviving spouse, Death Benefits will be paid to any surviving children under the age of 18.

DEDUCTIBLE - Amount of loss the policyholder pays in a claim. The policyholder is liable to pay the Deductible before the insurance company is obligated to pay the claim.

DEPOSIT PREMIUM - The premium paid at the beginning of the policy that provides for future premium adjustments based on an estimate of the final premium.

DIVIDEND - A payment made to the policyholder by an insurance company out of its surplus or net worth.

DATE OF INJURY (DOI) - The date upon which the accident occurred that caused the injury.

E

EARNED PREMIUM - The pro-rata portion of a written premium applicable to the expired portion of the policy term for which the insurance was in effect.

EFFECTIVE DATE - The date that coverage begins on an insurance policy.

EMPLOYER'S FIRST REPORT OF INJURY - A report that employers are required to file with their workers' compensation carriers when one of their employees is injured on the job.

EMPLOYER'S LIABILITY - Applies to bodily injury by accident or bodily injury by disease. The bodily injury must arise out of and in the course of employment. Bodily injury also applies to resulting death.

ENDORSEMENT - A written amendment attached to a policy modifying the terms of the insurance contract. The modification is only valid with the agreement of the insured, unless it is undoubtedly made solely for the benefit of the insured.

ESTIMATED PREMIUM - The premium on a term policy calculated using estimated payroll exposure.

EXPENSE CONSTANT - A flat charge added to small account premiums in order to cover the cost of issuing and servicing the policy.

EXPENSE RATIO - The percentage of premium used to pay for the acquisition, writing, and servicing of a policy. The Expense Ratio is equal to underwriting expenses divided by the written premium. The Expense Ratio effectively reveals how much it actually costs the insurance company to write the premiums.

EXPERIENCE MODIFICATION FACTOR (X-MOD) - Modifies a premium to reflect the loss experience of a policyholder compared with payroll exposure over the same time period. The modifier increases or decreases the current premium depending on how the actual exposure and losses, for the past three years, compare with expected losses for the same amount of exposure.

EXPIRATION DATE - The date coverage ends on an insurance policy.

EXPOSURE - Being subject to the possibility of a loss.

EXTRATERRITORIALITY - A provision in workers' compensation insurance law that extends protection to an employee that is injured in a state other than his state of hire.

F

FACULTATIVE REINSURANCE - Applies to part or all of a single policy, giving the primary insurer and the reinsurer the faculty or option to accept or reject the policy to be reinsured.

FINAL PREMIUM - Final Premium is calculated after a policy has expired and is calculated using actual payroll exposure.

FREQUENCY - The number of claims occurring over a period of time. May be based on accident year or policy year for an individual policy, a group of policies, or all policies.

G

GOVERNING CLASSIFICATION - A workers' compensation class code that has the most payroll exposure and generally describes the main business operation of the employer. The Governing Classification may not be a standard exception unless there are no other class codes other than the standard exceptions.

I

IMPAIRMENT RATING - Established by a claimant's physician to quantify a physical disability, typically reflecting the percentage of the claimant's whole body impairment. The Impairment Rating is determined by medical examinations using standard American Medical Association (AMA) guidelines. Individual states may have additional guidelines that supersede the AMA guidelines.

INCURRED BUT NOT REPORTED (IBNR) - Covered losses that occurred but have not yet been reported to the primary insurance company. A reserve is set up to account for this unknown liability, to more accurately reflect expected losses.

INCURRED BUT UNPAID BENEFITS (IBUB) - The general liability accounts that reflect the reserves currently booked to pay any future liabilities on outstanding claims and IBNR claims.

IN-FORCE - Reflects the exposure for which an insurance company is providing insurance coverage when a policy is active and coverage is extended.

INDEMNITY - Compensation for a loss.

INDEMNITY CLAIM - Includes payments and reserves for lost wages and medical expenses when an injured worker is out of work long enough to receive compensation for lost wages.

INDEPENDENT CONTRACTOR - An individual who does a job for another individual, or company, according to a contract and is not an employee of the individual or company. An independent contractor typically has significantly more control (independence) of how and when the work is completed than an employee would have.

INDEPENDENT MEDICAL EXAMINATION (IME) - An examination of an injured worker by a physician selected by the insurance company. It is generally done to determine the appropriateness of a course of treatment, or to provide an evaluation of permanent impairment.

INSTALLMENT PREMIUM - Partial payment of a premium made by the policyholder for coverage on a term policy. Determined by dividing the estimated premium into smaller amounts at set intervals during the policy period.

INFORMATION PAGE - The portion of a workers' compensation policy that describes a risk, It includes the insured's name and address, policy term, premiums and amount of coverage.

INSURANCE - The transfer of risk from one party (insured) to another (insurer), in which the insurer agrees to pay the insured (or their representative) an amount of money, or service, for losses sustained from an unexpected event, during a period of time for which the insured makes a premium payment to the insurer.

INSURANCE COMMISSIONER - The official of a state charged with the duty of enforcing its Insurance laws. Also commonly called the Superintendent of Insurance or Director of Insurance.

INVESTMENT INCOME - Money earned from invested assets. An insurance company's invested assets usually include reserves and policyholder surplus.

L

LONG-TAIL LINE - A line of insurance coverage where the occurrence and reporting of a loss and the payout of the claim is often spread out over a relatively long period of time. The unspecificity of the actual length of the time makes it difficult to determine the value of the claim when the claim is first reported.

LOSS - The amount an insurer is obligated to pay because of an insured event. Also defined as an injury caused by an event covered by an insurance company.

LOSS ADJUSTMENT EXPENSES (LAE) - All of the costs associated with the settlement of a claim, other than adjusting and other expenses.

LOSS CONVERSION FACTOR (LCF) - A multiplier used to calculate the premium of a retrospectively rated policy to include the cost of settling claims. Incurred losses are multiplied by the Loss Conversion Factor to obtain an amount equal to the incurred losses plus all loss adjustment expenses.

LOSS COST MULTIPLIER - A factor an insurance company files with the state insurance department to reflect the increase, or decrease of the state's rates that the insurance company will charge for workers' compensation.

LOSS RATIO - The percentage of losses plus loss adjustment expenses to the earned premium. The Loss Ratio exhibits how much premium was actually used to cover losses as well as the cost to settle the losses.

LOSS RUN - A report that lists the losses and expenses for claims filed on a policy over a given period of time. Also reports the premium earned for the period of time and the calculated loss ratio. Additionally, it provides a breakdown of losses by paid, reserves, and subrogation. In addition, losses are broken down further by type of loss. Only those expenses charged to a claim are listed on the loss run.

LOSSES INCURRED - An amount representing the losses paid plus the change in outstanding loss reserves within a given period of time. On an annual financial statement, the Losses Incurred are the losses paid during the year plus the loss reserves at the end of the year minus the loss reserves at the beginning of the year.

LOST TIME (OR "TIME LOSS") CLAIM - A claim in which an injured worker is unable to work for a period of time, as determined by a doctor. These claims typically involve the payment of disability benefits, in addition to medical costs and other expenses.

M

MANUAL PREMIUM - The premium before the experience modification and any premium discounts. Calculated by multiplying the exposure by the Manual Rate.

MANUAL RATE - The rate commonly used to calculate the premium on a policy. The Manual Rate is equal to the state rate multiplied by the appropriate loss cost multiplier (preferred, standard, non-standard) that was initially filed with the state insurance commissioner.

MAXIMUM MEDICAL IMPROVEMENT (MMI) - The maximum level of medical improvement to an injured worker's condition. Once a claimant obtains MMI, it is therefore accepted that medical improvements in the future will be minimal.

MEDICAL CASE MANAGEMENT - Professional services provided for the evaluation, monitoring and coordination of medical treatment for claims with specific diagnosis or requiring high-cost, extensive services.

MEDICAL ONLY CLAIM - A claim that includes payments only for medical expenses. It occurs when an injured worker was not out of work long enough to receive compensation for lost wages.

MINIMUM PREMIUM - The smallest possible premium charged for coverage during an annual period.

MODIFIED PREMIUM - The premium reflected after the adjustment for Experience Modification.

MONOPOLISTIC STATE FUND - State- operated insurance company that is the only provider of workers' compensation insurance in that state. No other insurance entities are permitted to write workers' compensation insurance in these states. There are currently four Monopolistic State Funds: North Dakota, Ohio, Washington and Wyoming.

MUTUAL INSURANCE COMPANY - A company owned and controlled by its policyholders. A Mutual Insurance Company's surplus may be distributed to the policyholders in the form of dividends.

N

NATIONAL ASSOCIATION OF INSURANCE COMMISSIONERS (NAIC) - Composed of state insurance commissioners to promote uniformity by drafting regulations and model legislation. The NAIC has achieved considerable multistate uniformity through their annual statement, which insurance companies rely on for financial reporting.

NATIONAL COUNCIL ON COMPENSATION INSURANCE (NCCI) - An organization comprising of insurance companies that write workers' compensation insurance. The NCCI collects statistics to establish rate structures in order to file rating plans with state insurance commissioners. The NCCI also maintains policy information and calculates X-mods for these policies.

NEGLIGENCE - Failure to take the care that a reasonably prudent party usually takes, whether by omission or commission, in a given situation, resulting in harm to another.

NET - Calculated after the application of an offset. Premium, net of reinsurance, is direct premium plus assumed premium, less ceded premium. Losses, net of reinsurance, is direct losses plus assumed losses, less ceded losses.

NET INVESTMENT INCOME - The total earned from invested assets minus investment expenses. An insurance company's invested assets typically reflect reserves and policyholder surplus.

NET INVESTMENT INCOME RATIO - The ratio of Net Investment Income to Net Earned Premiums.

NEW BUSINESS - The written premium from a business that has been in existence for less than 12 months.

NON-ADMITTED ASSETS - Any assets not considered by a state insurance department in determining the financial condition of an insurance company.

NOT OTHERWISE CLASSIFIED (NOC) - A class code term used to denote that a policyholder's operations cannot be classified more specifically.

O

OCCURRENCE - The result of a repeated exposure or event that unexpectedly causes loss or damage.

OPERATING RATIO - The combined ratio minus the net investment income ratio.

OWNER CONTROLLED INSURANCE PROGRAM (OCIP) - An insurance program usually written to cover large construction projects in which all **labour** performed under the contract is covered. The program usually includes insurance policies covering workers' compensation and general liability. Commonly called "wrap-up" policies.

P

PAID LOSSES - Total losses paid by an insurance company.

PAYMENT PLANS - Payment of premium in periodic **installments**, usually monthly.

PAYROLL EXPOSURE - The amount of possible loss to which an employer's workers are subject. Used to calculate the amount of premium due on a workers' compensation insurance policy.

PERMANENT DISABILITY RATINGS (PDR) - A rating range from 0% to 100% based on a number of factors (i.e., claimant's age, occupation, and the extent of disability) and corresponds to a fixed number of weeks of compensation. Zero percent signifies no reduction of earning capacity, while 100% represents permanent total disability. A rating between 0% and 100% represents Permanent Partial Disability.

PERMANENT PARTIAL DISABILITY (PPD) - An injured worker that has a Permanent Impairment Rating of less than 100% after the Maximum Medical Improvement has been reached. Benefits for PPD are paid over a specified period of time, depending on the severity of the permanent impairment.

PERMANENT TOTAL DISABILITY (PTD) - Refers to an injured worker whose injuries have rendered him permanently unable to perform the kind of work for which he is qualified, and who cannot perform other work that is reasonably available. In most, but not all cases, benefits for PTD are paid for the rest of the injured worker's life.

PHYSICIAN'S FIRST REPORT OF WORK INJURY - A report that a physician files with a workers' compensation carrier after an injured worker's initial examination by the physician after the accident.

POLICIES IN FORCE - Used to calculate claims frequency,

Policies In Force is the total number of policies that are active at any' given point in time.

POLICY PERIOD - The amount of time during which a policy is effective or in force.

POLICY YEAR - The year after the inception date of a policy.

POLICY YEAR EXPERIENCE - The matching of Policy Year Losses with Policy Year Premiums. Policy Year Experience changes as losses develop and premium finalizes.

POLICY YEAR LOSSES - The total combined losses on policies within a given policy year. Policy Year Losses for a given year change as claims develop. The ultimate Policy Year Losses is known once all claims that occurred during the given policy year are settled.

POLICY YEAR PREMIUM - The combined premium from policies within a given policy year. Policy Year Premium for a given year changes as premium adjusts in subsequent years. The ultimate Policy Year Premium is known once all premium adjustments are finalized. Policy Year Premium includes the entire premium for a policy in the policy year.

POLICYHOLDER ACQUISITION COSTS - The expenses incurred by an insurance company directly relating to writing a policy.

POLICYHOLDER SURPLUS - The excess of an insurance company's assets above its legal obligations to pay benefits to its policyholders and claimants.

PREFERRED PROVIDER ORGANIZATION(PPO) - A formally organized entity consisting of hospitals, physicians, and other healthcare providers. A PPO allows insurance companies to negotiate directly for healthcare services at a lower price than would normally be charged.

PREMIUM - The price paid by a policyholder to an insurance company in return for insurance coverage.

PREMIUM AUDIT - An examination of a policyholder's operations, books and records by a premium specialist to determine the actual insurance exposure of the coverages provided.

PREMIUM REFUND - The amount of premium that has been collected over and above the final earned premium that is returned to the policyholder.

PREMIUM RESERVES - There are two types: 1. Premium Earned But Not Received (EBNR) - Premium due but not received by the end of the accounting period. 2. Unearned Premium Reserve (UEPR)- Premium paid for coverage beyond the end of the accounting period.

PREMIUM SPECIALIST - An individual who does premium audits for an insurance company. Also known as a Premium Auditor.

PREMIUM TAX - Payment made to a state, or municipality, by an insurance company based on a written premium.

PROCEEDS - The benefits payable under an insurance policy.

PROFESSIONAL EMPLOYER ORGANIZATION (PEO) - A company providing outsourced insurance benefits and human resource consulting to other companies. The insurance benefits are provided as part of a group policy. Also known as

Employee Leasing.

PROSPECTIVE RATING - The determining of premium rates based on loss experience over a specified past period of time.

R

RECOVERIES - Amounts received as reimbursement for paid losses. Recoveries include amounts from overpayments, subrogation and second injury fund.

REINSURANCE - An agreement whereby the reinsurer agrees to compensate the ceding company for all or part of the losses that the ceding company may experience under the policy or policies which it has issued.

REINSURED - An insurance company that has placed reinsurance risk with a reinsurer in the business of buying reinsurance. Also known as a ceding company.

REINSURER - A company that assumes the liability of another by way of reinsurance.

RETROSPECTIVELY RATED POLICY - A policy where the final premium is determined based on a formula using the current policy period's incurred losses. The formula elements and factors are included on the policy. Initially, premium is estimated using expected losses. After policy expiration, the premium is adjusted using actual losses. Retrospectively Rated Policies are similar to self-insurance due to the risk assumed by the policyholder, but unlike self-insurance the assumed risk under a Retrospectively Rated Policy is limited.

RISK - Refers to the individual or organization insured and also the uncertainty of financial loss.

RISK BASED CAPITAL REQUIREMENTS (RBC) - These are minimum capital standards that an insurance company must meet based on an assessment of the risk associated with the insurance company's operations.

RISK UNIT - The employee covered by workers' compensation insurance or the intrinsic item insured.

S

SCHEDULE CREDIT/DEBIT - A premium discount (or surcharge) available to policyholders. Schedule rating provides a discount or surcharge based on the policyholder's workplace safety programs and risk characteristics.

SECOND INJURY FUND - Set up by states to encourage companies to hire workers who have been handicapped by a prior workplace injury. When a worker has a second injury, after being hired by another company, the current company's insurance company is responsible for only the costs of the second injury. The Second Injury Fund will pay the difference between the total costs and the costs of the second injury. Second Injury Funds are usually funded by general state revenues or by assessments on workers' compensation companies.

SELF-INSURANCE - Protecting against losses by setting aside a company's own money, rather than purchasing an insurance policy. By being self-insured, a company saves expenses that an insurance company charges for acquisition, premium tax and general overhead. Typically, self-insured companies use a third-party administrator to administer their claims.

SOLVENCY - The minimum standard of financial well-being for an insurance company, where assets exceed liabilities. State insurance laws require insurance regulators to step in when the solvency of an insurance company is threatened and proceed with rehabilitation or liquidation.

STANDARD EXCEPTION - Refers to certain employee groups rated separately instead of being included under the main class code. The Standard Exception, for workers' compensation, are 8810 Clerical Office, 8742 Outside Sales, and 7380 Drivers, unless the main class code description states that one of these employee groups is included under the main class code.

STANDARD PREMIUM - The premium after adjustment for experience modification, safety credits/debits, schedule credits/debits, and association credits, but prior to adjustment for size and discount and expense constant. Standard Premium is used in retrospective rating to calculate the basic premium, maximum and minimum.

STATUTORY ACCOUNTING PRINCIPLES (SAP) - The rules of accounting and reporting required by state insurance law that must be followed by insurance companies in submitting their financial statements to state insurance departments.

STOP LOSS PROVISION - A policy provision on a retrospectively rated policy that limits the loss amount for any individual claim that is included in calculating the retrospective premium. A Stop Loss Provision is an additional election, made by the policyholder, for which they are given a higher premium factor.

SUBROGATION - An insurance company's right to take legal action against a third party responsible for a loss to the insured to which a claim has been paid.

T

TEMPORARY PARTIAL DISABILITY (TPD) - An injured worker's status prior to reaching maximum medical improvement has been reached, during which time he can perform some work, usually in a modified capacity or at fewer hours per day. Benefits for TPD are paid until the worker is released to full duty work, or has reached maximum medical improvement.

TEMPORARY TOTAL DISABILITY (TTD) - An injured worker's status prior to reaching maximum medical improvement has been reached, during which time he is unable to perform any work at all, as determined by a physician. Benefits for TED are paid until the worker is released to return to work, or has reached maximum medical improvement.

TERM PAYROLL REPORT - A payroll report sent by a termed policyholder that describes the actual exposure that occurred during the term period. The report is used to calculate final premium.

TERM POLICY - An insurance policy that is written with an established expiration date. Coverage only continues if the policy is renewed. The policy is written with estimated premium based on estimated payroll exposures.

TERMS - The provisions described in an insurance policy.

THIRD-PARTY ADMINISTRATOR (TPA) - The performance of the claims functions related to an insurance plan by a company that is not an original party to the insurance plan.

TOTAL INCURRED LOSS - An amount that represents the expected payout on a claim over the life of the claim. Incurred loss is equal to net paid losses (paid losses less recoveries) plus reserves.

TOTAL RESERVES - All total reserves of outstanding claims, whether known or unknown. Includes case reserves, IBNR reserves, and bulk reserves. Total Reserves also includes reserves for loss adjustment expenses.

TRADE ASSOCIATION - A group of companies in a similar industry that is organized to obtain cost savings. Each Trade Association generally endorses one insurance company as its workers' compensation insurance carrier of choice in exchange for premium discounts.

TREATY REINSURANCE - The reinsurance of only part of the policies written by an insurance company. Treaty Reinsurance may be by participating type, where the insurance company and reinsurer share the risk based on a pro rata share agreement, or by excess type, where the reinsurer reimburses the insurance company for claims that exceed a predetermined loss amount. Compare this with facultative reinsurance.

ULTIMATE NET LOSS - The total payments resulting from a claim over the life of this claim, plus all related expenses, less recoveries and reinsurance. Total payment reflects that the loss has fully developed, and all loss payments are known.

U

UNDERWRITER - An individual who decides which applicants for insurance coverage are accepted or rejected, what coverage is provided, and what price to charge for this coverage.

UNDERWRITING PROFIT OR LOSS - An insurance company's profit or loss strictly from its insurance operations. This is in contrast to investment operations.

UNEARNED PREMIUM - The portion of the premium applicable to the unexpired period of the policy.

UTILIZATION REVIEW - The process that determines the medical necessity of services and procedures that have been submitted as necessary for a particular claimant.

W

WORKERS' COMPENSATION INSURANCE - Insurance coverage for employees that is required by law in cases of injury or death due to an occupational accident, regardless of the employer's negligence.

WORKERS' COMPENSATION UNIT REPORT - A statistical representation that provides information about payroll, premium and losses for a specific policy and state.

WRITTEN PREMIUM - Refers to the entire amount or premium written during a described period regardless of which portions have and have not been earned.

CHAPTER 5

Cyber-liability, the New Information Highway Robbery, Data Breach, and Identity Theft - If You Think Credit Card Companies are Protecting You in Case of Fraud, Think Again!

Welcome to the new information highway (robbery). Everyone accepts credit cards these days. With debit Visa and MasterCard, it has become virtually unnecessary to carry cash or checks. If you take credit cards (and who doesn't?), you have a legal responsibility to protect your customers' private financial data. But, what if you get hacked? I have a client who owns six franchises throughout Southern California. She got a call from MasterCard one day letting her knows that her system had been broken into, and customer credit card information had been used fraudulently. Much to her surprise, her MasterCard agreement required her to pay for the cost of a forensic expert to investigate each location, and find out what exactly happened. The cost? $2500 per location. $15,000. Start there. When this is all said and done, she will likely have to pay much, much more. Save your a$$ets.

Visa and MasterCard don't protect you in case of a data breach. You can be held responsible for, not only the direct damage if your customer has money stolen, but also the cost of investigation, notifying ALL your customers of the breach, defense, the damage to your reputation, and on and on. In this chapter you will find essential information on how to protect yourself from robbers as you cruise down the new information highway.

The Questions Clients Mostly Ask

1. What is Data Breach Insurance?

When you accept credit cards, you have a responsibility to keep your customer's private information secure from outside hackers. If you do get hacked, and your customer's information is stolen, you may be liable for direct damage, as well as a myriad of other costs such as credit monitoring, restoring your reputation, forensic investigations, etc. Data breach insurance pays these costs.

2. Doesn't my current credit processor cover this?

Your credit card processor (Visa, MasterCard, etc.) does not cover you for data breach.

3. Is this coverage part of my restaurant package policy, or is it sold separately?

It is a separate coverage and is not a part of your standard restaurant package.

4. What is the average cost of a policy?

The average cost of a separate policy is about $500 per year, but can vary depending on limits and other factors.

5. What are the chances of having a data breach, and what are the costs that could be occurred?

The chances of having a breach depend greatly on the steps a business takes to prevent one. Having a firewall in place along with proper router configuration, software updates, anti-virus programs and updates, and records retention policies can all greatly reduce your business' chances of being hacked, but nothing is fool-proof. For that reason cyber-liability insurance is becoming increasingly important to cover the potential costs such as:

- the direct loss sustained by misuse of a customer's credit card information

- the cost of a forensic investigation to determine what caused the breach and who, exactly, has been affected

- notification to your customer's of a breach and the cost of credit monitoring for them

- defense costs

- the cost of restoring your business' reputation

6. Really, how much can this type of claim cost me?

The forensic investigation alone can cost thousands. That's only one part. A cyber-liability claim has the potential to cost hundreds of thousands or much more before all is said and done. Think about all the INDIVIDUAL credit card transactions you process in a day, and you'll have some idea of how much a potential claim can cost your business.

7. Can this shutdown my business for a period time?

Definitely. Customers today expect to be able to use a credit card to pay for their meal. Many people do not carry cash at all, or a very small amount. If you are not able to process credit card transactions for a time because of a breach, this can greatly affect your ability to stay open.

8. Where do I get more information?

Your broker can provide more information on the cost and coverage of a cyber-liability policy.

9. How can I prevent a claim?

You can reduce the chances of a claim by having a firewall in place along with proper router configuration, software updates, anti-virus programs and updates, and records retention policies, but nothing is fool-proof as hackers get more and more sophisticated. This is why it is a cyber-liability policy should be looked at as an essential part of your insurance plan.

10. How do I report a claim?

Report a claim to your broker as soon as you become aware or are notified you've been hacked.

The Questions Clients Should be Asking

1. What services, programs or companies can I use to be proactive and avoid this type of claim?

A network security company can be very valuable in avoiding a cyber-liability claim. Make sure the company reviews your network security protocols, and that it scans and backs up your network daily.

2. What contract should I fully read to understand my responsibilities?

You need to read and understand your credit card processing agreement with VISA, MasterCard, etc., BEFORE a breach happens to make sure you have the necessary safeguards in place.

3. Is there a choice of coverage's and deductibles?

Yes. Limits up to $2,000,000 are available and deductibles of $1000 or higher. Your broker can help you tailor a policy to meet your needs.

4. After a breach can I pick my own forensic investigator?

The Forensic investigator must be approved by the credit card issuing authority (VISA, MasterCard, etc.).

5. Can just a firewall installed avoid data breach?

A firewall is a great place to start, but you also need secure routing configuration, anti-virus software, proper records retention procedures, just to name a few.

6. What is the difference between policies and companies?

Cyber-liability policies vary greatly from company to company in coverage and cost. Your broker can select and recommend the best company and coverage for the individual needs of your business.

7. Do any of the Companies have any type of hotline?

Yes they do. This is an extremely important added benefit in your selection of a company. Ask your broker if a company that he or she is recommending offers a hotline service.

Cyber Liability Checklist:

___ I have reviewed my credit card processing agreements, and am aware of my requirements and obligations.

___ I have security in place for my electronic systems such as a firewall, and an up-to-date anti-virus program.

___ I have a records retention policy in place outlining how long information will be stored, and when and how it will be securely disposed of.

___ I have a cyber-liability insurance policy in place that provides coverage in case of a data breach.

CHAPTER 6

High Risk Outside Your Premises - The Hidden Dangers

Your customers come to you for a good meal and a good time, and you take care of them well and send them on their way. That should be the end of it, right? Not always. I had a client whose customer left their restaurant on the beach and made a u-turn on the Pacific Coast Highway. An illegal maneuver, by the way. When the very major accident happened, the customer started naming everyone in the lawsuit including the city for not warning against u-turns, all the other drivers on the road, and our restaurant because the valet did not warn the customer about making a u-turn when he handed over the keys. Anything can happen. Be protected.

When it's clear they have a few too many, you offer to call them a cab. Makes sense, right? You're trying to be a good Samaritan. I have a client who did this, but the guy made his way back to the restaurant to pick up his car before he'd sobered up. He hit someone. The restaurant was found partly to blame due to dram shop laws. Anything can happen. Be protected.

When they'd rather you come to them, delivery is a great, convenient service for your customers. You send your employee out with his car full of ribs to take to a picnic never thinking anything out of the ordinary will happen. Usually it doesn't. But, one day the unthinkable happened to my client. His driver hit a pedestrian. It was just a freak accident. The restaurant's policy paid their limit of $1,000,000. Anything can happen. Be protected.

In major cities, a valet is a must. Not just at fancy places anymore, but everywhere. Parking is expensive and scarce and your customers would just rather not bother. Be careful, though! If you don't have the proper insurance protections in place, offering valet service could be very expensive for you. I have a client whose valet assured him he had liability coverage, he even gave my client a very professional looking certificate of insurance. It was only after the valet hit a pedestrian that my client found out all the insurance information the valet provided was bogus. The lawsuit resulted in such financial devastation that my client had to close his doors. "Additional insured." Make sure you're one on the valet's policy, make sure they prove it to you, and make sure it's valid. Don't be the client of mine that was not careful about this, whose valet opened a customer's car door in front of a person on a bike and who had to pay their own defense costs out of pocket. Anything can happen. Be protected.

You know you need insurance coverage for all the things that can happen at your restaurant, but your business likely doesn't stop there. Maybe you deliver, or cater away from your premises. Maybe you offer a valet service. This chapter will explain how you can protect yourself from some of the things that can happen away from your premises.

The Questions Clients Mostly Ask

1. What is hired and non-owned auto coverage?

Your liability policy does not provide coverage for your business arising from your employee's use of a vehicle. If your business owns vehicles, you can get coverage through a commercial auto policy. If however, your business occasionally rents a vehicle or your employees occasionally use their own vehicles in the course of their duties, you can get liability coverage through the use of a hired and non-owned auto endorsement. Hired means rented, and non-owned means not owned by the business (your employee uses their own car registered to them personally). Note, though, that special non-owned auto coverage is required if the employee use is for delivery or transporting customers.

2. How do I get coverage for hired and non-owned autos?

Generally, by an endorsement to your general liability policy. A special non-owned auto policy is required, though, when employees use their own vehicles to deliver or transport customers.

3. What is the difference between commercial and personal auto?

Whether a vehicle should be covered by commercial or personal auto insurance depends on many factors. If the vehicle is registered to a business, it generally must be covered by a commercial policy. If it is registered to an individual, then it is personal auto. Another factor is use. Personal auto policies exclude coverage while a vehicle is being used to transport persons or property for a fee. The size of the vehicle is also a consideration. Large trucks usually fall outside the definition of an auto in the personal auto policy. Your broker will be able to determine whether a vehicle should be covered by a commercial or personal auto policy. The coverages afforded by the two policies are vastly different, and cost alone should not be the primary concern in making this determination. You don't want to get in an accident only to find out you don't have the coverage you need.

4. How do I protect myself when I have a valet service or hire a valet employee?

If you contract directly with a valet service, you should make sure they have a liability policy in place with limits of coverage of at least $1,000,000, and that you are named on their policy as additional insured. Ask the valet service to provide you with a certificate of insurance. If you hire valet employees, you need a type of coverage called Garage Keepers Legal Liability. This provides protection if your valet employee damages a customer's vehicle while operating it. Hint: operating is usually taken to mean driving as well as being "in, on, or around." The fact the customer's car is not moving does not mean Garage Keepers Coverage is not needed if it is damaged. It will also cover your liability if a valet driver causes damage to another vehicle or injures a pedestrian. Ask your broker about adding this to your policy.

5. What coverage is needed for delivery and what am I responsible for?

If your employee uses their own vehicle for delivery, and is in an accident, you may be partially liable as the employer. A special non-owned auto policy for delivery is required to provide the coverage you need. Ask your broker for more information on this type of policy.

6. Am I responsible when my employee uses their own vehicle during work hours?

If they are using their vehicle at your direction, you could be partially liable as their employer. Make sure you have non-owned auto coverage if your employees use their own vehicles for business purposes.

7. Doesn't my current package policy cover the delivery exposure?

No. Your general liability policy specifically excludes nearly all uses of a vehicle. A non-owned auto endorsement will provide the coverage you need and for delivery, a special separate non-owned policy for delivery is required.

8. What is the premium based on for the non-owned auto for delivery policy, and is it expensive?

The premium is generally based on your gross receipts derived from delivery activities and will vary based on how much delivery you do. The motor vehicle records of your drivers can also be a factor, and it is important to hire delivery drivers with good driving records.

9. How do I reduce the chances of a claim, and are there any secrets in hiring employees for delivery or a valet service?

First, make sure you have a non-owned auto policy for delivery in place. Next, don't offer a guaranteed delivery time to your customers. This may encourage your drivers to go too fast and pose a higher accident risk. It is also important to check the motor vehicle records of your drivers regularly and make sure they maintain good driving records.

If you hire a valet company, make sure they have liability insurance and that your restaurant is named as additional insured. Require that the valet company provide you a certificate of insurance proving this before they do any work for you. Contact the insurance company and/or broker listed on the certificate to confirm the policy is in force.

10. How do I insure special events or catering?

Make sure your broker is aware of the fact that you offer catering, and whether it is on and/or off your premises. Your property/liability policy will generally cover catering events on your premises automatically, but catering off premises might require additional coverage. He/she will be able to make sure you have what you need including:

- coverage for any vehicles owned by or rented to you for off premises catering

- coverage for liability arising from your employees use of their own vehicles for delivery or catering

- liquor liability if you will be serving liquor at the event

- adequate coverage for your business property that is

taken off premises for catering

- adequate coverage for liability claims from food poisoning, chipped tooth claims, spills, and burns, etc.

11. Am I responsible if a customer is intoxicated and gets into an accident on the way home?

Many states, including California, have laws on the books that hold a business owner responsible if they serve liquor, if they serve it to an intoxicated person, and if that person gets into an accident after leaving the premises. These are commonly referred to as "dram shop laws." Be sure you have liquor liability as part of your general liability package. Liquor liability provides coverage for the business owner in this type of situation.

12. What coverage do I need if I have property, like a sign, away from my premises?

Your property/liability package has very limited coverage for property that is usually kept away from your premises, like a sign announcing your restaurant a mile or so out on the highway. Make sure your broker knows of any such property so he/she can increase your limits of coverage for off premises property.

Risks Outside of Premises Checklist:

___   I have obtained motor vehicle records for delivery drivers, if any, and reviewed them. I have written criteria regarding acceptable and unacceptable driving records for drivers (your insurance agent can help you with this).

___   I have non-owned auto coverage in place specifically for delivery, if any, that protects me in case a driver is involved in an accident driving their own personal vehicle.

___   I have commercial auto coverage in place for vehicles owned by the business, if any.

___   I have proper coverage for valet drivers, and if valets are independent contractors, I have obtained a certificate of insurance naming my business as additional insured and have verified the policy is in force (your insurance agent can help you with this).

___   I have liquor liability coverage to protect me for my legal responsibilities if I serve liquor.

___   I have adequate coverage for any business property, such as a sign, normally kept at a location away from my premises.

CHAPTER 7

Costly Natural and Not So Natural Disasters - Are You Prepared?

The experts say California is due for the "big one." I sure hope not, but I personally find worrying about things I have no control over to be stressful and overwhelming. All we can do is be prepared.

A big misconception about earthquake insurance is that it will only cover total destruction of the structure because of the high deductible. Our client, an Italian restaurant in North Hollywood, was damaged in the quake of 1991, but the building still stood. The damage was severe enough, though, to close the restaurant for almost five months (the city and county permit process alone can take a toll on any business). In addition to the structural damage, my client's collection of expensive imported wine was gone. He lost some other contents, continued to pay payroll for key employees, continued to pay very high rent and other operating expenses, and let's not forget he had no income during the time he was closed, and it took some time for business to resume after he opened back up. I can remember how grateful he was when he was able to recover over $400,000 from his earthquake insurance policy. Since 1991, companies that provide earthquake insurance have steadily increased their minimum deductibles, so it is important to plan an emergency fund to cover this gap. Don't wait until it's too late.

Remember hurricane Katrina? I have a client with operations in many states including Louisiana and Mississippi. Our policy covered the wind damage that closed his restaurants for months. We were able to protect his family business and loss of income. Some of his friends in the same areas weren't so lucky. Strangely, their policies excluded wind damage. Be aware of inherent geographic hazards and don't take mother nature lightly.

Your property and liability policy is comprehensive, and does a great job of protecting you. Some natural disasters, however, are so enormous in scope and potential financial devastation that insurance companies have to exclude them from coverage. If they didn't, everyone's premiums would have to skyrocket, even those who don't reside in a disaster prone area. This chapter will explain what these risks are and how to fill any gaps you may have in your coverage.

The Questions Clients Mostly Ask

1. Does the Restaurant property/liability cover against loss of income due to riots?

The restaurant property/liability policy, in general, does not exclude riot or civil commotion. This means such incidents would be covered. Acts of war and acts of terrorism are generally not covered. Terrorism coverage can usually be added back to a policy by endorsement.

2. Do I need Earthquake Insurance?

Your standard property policy does not cover damage resulting from earthquakes. Damage from a quake can be catastrophic. It is highly recommended that you purchase, or at least look into, earthquake coverage to protect your business, as well as your personal, assets.

3. Is earthquake insurance expensive and what does it cover?

Earthquake insurance rates depend on where a building is located, as well as what it is made of and how old it is. Newer wood frame or stucco buildings that are retrofitted are far less expensive to insure than older masonry buildings that are not. Earthquake policies can cover damage to buildings, business property, and loss of business income. Because of the catastrophic nature of the damage an earthquake can cause, they usually have very high deductibles. The deductibles can range from 5 to 25 percent of the insured value.

4. What constitutes a flood?

A flood is usually defined as complete or partial inundation of normally dry land areas by water from any source. Your standard property policy excludes damage from flooding, as well as any water that comes up from underground such as backup from a sewer or drain system. The policy can be endorsed to include water backup coverage, but a flood requires a specific and separate flood policy.

5. What is the difference between rain and flood?

Flood is the inundation of normally dry land by water. The water can, and frequently does come from excessive rain, but doesn't have to. Water damage caused by rain can be covered if first some portion of the building is damaged and lets the rain in. For example, if high winds cause roof damage, and that damage allows rain into a building, then the rain damage would be covered. Flood damage is not covered by a property policy. A specific separate flood policy would be needed.

6. Do all policies cover against hurricanes and wind damage?

Wind damage, including the wind caused by a hurricane, is covered by a standard property policy. The only exception may be in certain hurricane-prone areas of certain states where insurance companies have specifically excluded wind damage. California is not one of those states.

7. What do you do in case of a natural disaster claim?

In the event of damage to your property, it is your responsibility to secure the property from further damage when possible. Document the damage and take photos whenever practical. Contact your broker as soon as you can describe what has been damaged, how the damage occurred, and when it occurred. Forward any repair bills and estimates, including bills, for anything you did to protect property to your broker. If you have to close your business due to the damage, you will need to provide current and historic financial data to the adjuster in order to have the business income portion of the claim settled. It is a good idea to start gathering that information right away. Sales and expense journals, and P&L statements are a good start. Remember you will need to provide these for the last few months before the claim, and probably also for the same period the prior year.

8. What is the best record I could keep to assist the claims process?

A video inventory of your property is very helpful. Keep receipts and copies of invoices for all purchases. Take photos or video of any damage as soon as practical. Contact your broker right away and describe the property damaged, what caused the damage, when the damage happened, and provide copies of any estimates you've obtained. Also, keep records of any expenses you incur to protect property from further damage. Some of this expense might be reimbursable. For business income claims the adjuster will generally need to see copies of sales journals and financial reports for a few months before the loss, as well as for the same period of time for the prior year.

9. For all the natural disasters what preventive measures could I do?

Earthquake – Make sure your building is retrofitted to minimize damage. Large appliances and shelving should be permanently affixed in such a way as to minimize the likelihood they will fall over in an earthquake.

Flood – If you feel there is a danger of flooding, move property and inventory up off the floor to prevent water damage. You should have a flood policy in force if you are in a flood risk area. Flood insurance is subject to a waiting period before it becomes effective, so don't wait until flood damage is imminent.

Wind – As soon as you hear of a high wind warning you should bring property indoors that is normally kept outdoors like furniture and tables on a patio. Bring in awnings to prevent damage in a wind storm. Board up or shutter windows if necessary. Make sure roofs are in good condition so they are less likely to suffer wind damage in a storm.

The Questions Clients Should be Asking

1. What coverage do I really need in an Earthquake policy?

If you own or are responsible for insuring a building, you should have building coverage. You should also insure tenant improvements if any. You should always cover business personal property and loss of business income.

2. Do I need to insure to full replacement value?

Yes. Not insuring to 100% of replacement value may result in a lower loss settlement even in the case of a partial loss. For example, a business has property worth $1,000,000, but only chooses to buy $500,000 coverage (50% of full replacement). The business has a claim for $50,000 to repair or replace some property. The insurance company would only pay 50% of that amount because the business is only insured for 50% of full replacement. This is called coinsurance.

3. What limit of flood insurance do I need, and what determines if I need flood insurance?

You should purchase flood insurance if you are in a flood

prone area, but flood insurance is available and is very affordable even when you're not. You should insure to 100% of replacement value, but flood insurance is a national government program even when it is administered by private companies and there are maximum limits of coverage that can be bought. There would not be any type of coinsurance penalty if you purchase the maximum limits available. <u>Flood insurance policies do not include business income coverage.</u>

4. What are the critical areas the claim adjuster will ask to determine if I get the full value of my restaurant in the case of a fire?

The adjuster will endeavor to determine the full replacement value of all property and check to see if you are insured to the proper limits to avoid a coinsurance penalty. You should always maintain 100% full replacement value limits on your property policy.

5. Will it cost me a lot more money to properly insure my restaurant with respects to natural disasters?

Premiums vary widely based on age and other characteristics of your building, location, insurance company, etc. Your broker can provide quotes at no cost to you.

6. I am in an older location, a historical landmark or a tightly controlled zoning area. What insurance considerations are there in these situations?

If your business suffers substantial damage, there may be zoning laws and building regulations in existence now that were not there at the time your building was built. It may be necessary to comply with new regulations that will increase the cost of repairs or replacement. It may also be necessary to demolish part of a building even though it was not damaged. The standard property policy does not cover any of this increased cost. If you are in an older building, a historical landmark, or in an area that has tightly controlled zoning regulations, you need to have Building Ordinance and Law Coverage including Increased Cost of Construction and Demolition Cost. Ask your broker to make sure you do, and that your limits are adequate to cover these additional expenses.

7. Is there truly a difference between companies covering natural disasters?

There are vast differences in rates and coverage among companies offering earthquake policies. Your broker should always make sure at each renewal that you have the best coverage at the most affordable cost available. Flood insurance is a little different. Flood policy forms, rules, underwriting, and rates are all set by the National Flood Insurance Program. Independent insurance companies may administer issuing policies, settling claims, and collecting premiums, but there is no difference in cost between companies for flood insurance. HOWEVER, there are ways to greatly reduce the cost of a flood insurance policy by, for example, providing certain documentation of a building's elevation, and not all brokers may be aware of them.

Natural Disasters Checklist:

___ I have a disaster preparedness plan in place that includes business continuation arrangements where feasible.

___ I have investigated the cost and benefits of earthquake coverage for my business property and loss of income.

___ I have investigated the cost and benefits of flood insurance for my business property, especially if my business is in a flood-prone area.

___ I have taken measures to protect my property from damage in the event of an earthquake such as retro-fitting and securing large appliances and shelving to keep them from falling over.

___ I have discussed the need for increased building ordinance and law coverage with my agent, especially if I am in an older building where zoning laws have changed since the building was originally built.

CHAPTER 8

Your Expert Team - Interviews with Business & Industry Experts

If you break your ankle, you wouldn't go to a general practitioner for casting (unless you're on an episode of "Survivor" in which case, he or she'd do just fine until you got home). You wouldn't go to an orthodontist to get a tooth filled (sure they could do it but it's not their bread and butter). If you need to set up estate planning, you wouldn't go to your neighbor who is a criminal attorney.

Trusting insurance for your business to an agent that mainly takes care of personal insurance but does some business insurance here and there is a potentially costly mistake. An expert is someone whose experience and years in the trenches have exposed him or her to a variety of different situations (although I'm still occasionally surprised). Experts study extensively in their field. They have a good idea of what you need now and the skills to anticipate some of your potential risks and exposures. Someone who calls himself or herself an expert is held to a higher standard, so do your due diligence when selecting your team. Choose someone who is a specialist in their area such as:

- estate planners

- a CPA that works with businesses

- tax attorneys who set up strategies to reduce your tax burden

- employment law attorneys

- an attorney who specializes in contracts and real estate

- an independent commercial insurance agent who is an expert in your particular business and who can represent many companies and is not beholden to just one

- a buying service that can reduce food and paper costs and track rebates

- a restaurant broker and expediter if you are buying or selling

All of these are very different and specialized fields. They should all be part of your team.

What follows are interviews with some of the top experts that specialize in restaurants and other businesses.

Interview 1

Mario Carron of Mario Carron Restaurant & Bar Brokerage

In their 35 years experience, Mario Carron, Inc. has sold and leased nearly 1200 food/bar establishments. They have sold more restaurants than any other company in the greater Los Angeles area. Mario is an expert at realistically pricing businesses based on current market conditions. He absolutely has his finger on the pulse of the food service industry in Southern California.

Interviewer: *Good Morning, we are sitting here with Mario Carron, our expert for today and we would like to welcome him to our session. Good Morning Mario.*

Mario Carron: *Good Morning. When you first called me up and you sent me this questionnaire, I thought about it and said, "What am I going to say?" Ever since the third quarter of 2008, my business, the restaurant business, the resale and restaurant business has been challenging, and it's continuing to get worse. So, what would you do if you were a parent, and your child said dad or mom, I want to open up a restaurant. Or mom and dad, I'd like to be a movie star. To go into the restaurant business today, you had better have a very clear cut business plan about how you're going to make it. You better know that business inside and out, and you are going to tell people who have never been in the restaurant business, "You want to go into the restaurant business, Fine. Go work for a major chain. Go work for the Cheesecake Factory, go work for Olive Garden. You've got to learn the business inside and out." Don't call up your broker and say that you're wife's a good cook and you want to open up a restaurant. No. Go and learn the business inside and out, and find a niche. You've got to find a niche where you can make it. Right now, the niches seem to be, especially in certain areas of Los Angeles, bar-oriented places. Heavy bar businesses dealing* *with yuppies, dealing with people who have high-disposable incomes. This appears to be where the money is.*

Interviewer: *So that brings us to a great question. What are the top five or seven secrets in order to be a successful restaurant business? You said one is that you've got to have your niche.*

Mario Carron: *One is you've got to have your niche. And you've got to have your business plan. Why are you going to be successful, why are you going to have a better taco, hamburger, better Italian food, why? Why are you going to better? And, maybe you are better; maybe you have better food, better quality. So, you've got to know the business inside and out, and you've got to find a location where that business plan is going to work. You've got to sign a lease that you can live with. Many of the leases today are absolutely ridiculous. I have a restaurant where one of the owners worked for Wolfgang Puck and had an incredible reputation. He opened a restaurant with a fabulous reputation. The restaurant is losing $10,000 a month. The rent is so impossible. It seats 40 people with an $11,000 rent. It is impossible. In some wealthy areas all these independent restaurants may look busy, but they aren't making any money. The rents are just too high.*

Interviewer: *So that is one of the big factors.*

Mario Carron: *Another thing you should have, you should deal with experts. In any business today, you've got to have an accountant, you should have an attorney to review all legal documents, leases, contracts, and everything should be reviewed by a professional. Many people sign leases and believe me, they don't know what they signed. They believe they have one thing, and then the read the lease and they have something entirely different. So, you've got to bank on professionals to help you along. And you have to be prepared to work very hard. You have to like the customers. As with any business, you have to love the business. You have to really love the work, love the business to* make it. You have to be realistic about what the real profit margins are. Capital investment in a restaurant can be mind-boggling. How much cushion do you have if your restaurant doesn't take off? Some restaurants take off in their first week. There was a restaurant in Calabasas, when they opened 30 years ago, it took two years before they could make a profit.

Interviewer: *Okay, so one factor is to have an emergency fund for at least a year?*

Mario Carron: *Absolutely. The number one failure rate today is that their concept is incorrect, they sign bad leases, they don't have enough working capital, and I think those are the biggest reasons for failure.*

Interviewer: *And they don't have experience?*

Mario Carron: *Yeah, if you don't know what you are doing, you're out. You asked me who you should trust when you buy a business. The answer is that you should trust no one but yourself. The broker is not your friend. The seller is not your friend. The landlord is not your friend. If you're buying a business based on the claims these people make, you've got to verify it. You've got to bring in accountants, and you've got to look at three years of financial statements. You should have professionals, especially an accountant, and attorney that reviews legal documents especially leases. They have to verify what they are selling. You would be stunned.*

Here's a story as an example:

Two guys called me up and they had a pizza restaurant for sale, and I asked them if they were making money and they said, yes. They said that they can prove on their taxes that they made $42,000 each. So, I said let's look at your books and records. They were nice gentlemen, intelligent gentlemen. I was looking at the books and said, "Well, wait a minute, where is the rent?", and they said, "We haven't paid rent in one year." If you factored the rent in, the guys aren't making profit, they were losing money. And, they nodded in agreement. How in god's name did you buy the place? Now these were smart guys. They came from high-tech business. They wanted to go into the restaurant business for a while, and they saw this restaurant that nets, I don't know, $200,000 a year. So, they met the broker, they met the seller. I asked them if they were shown the books and records and they said no. The books and records had shown that they (the former owners) were making no money, or even losing money, but they claimed that they had been skimming $200,000 a year off the top. Unbelievable, but they believed it. I told them to sue the broker, they won't and they can't even walk away because they owe SBA on their parent's home. I asked them how the landlord didn't kick them out. Well, apparently the landlord had a number of vacancies and was out of the country, they sent him letters and he never took action to get these guys removed. That's one of the most extreme cases I've ever heard of. Unbelievable.

Interviewer: *That's incredible. Okay, so we were talking about what to look for when purchasing existing business. The books have to be verified by a CPA. That makes sense, that makes a lot of sense. What are the overall costs when looking at existing restaurants, and what are the signs to back off.*

Mario Carron: *In the restaurant business? My daughter used to call it the smell test. When you go into the restaurant, what is your immediate impression of it? She would go into the ladies room and smell it. For example, this week I'm going to a restaurant in Redondo Beach. I said that I've got to see the inside. It hasn't been remodeled in 30 years. You can't go into a restaurant and just paint it over, make a few superficial changes. Those days are over. Renovations have to be spectacular. Most restaurants I sell today, you've got to gut them. Think about the sushi restaurant down the road. He hasn't done anything major, but he remodeled the whole front, but that one was relatively new. If you go into an old restaurant, god forbid you have to pull a permit. Here's what they do now, here's my recommendation. If you think you will have to pull* permits, by all means hire an expeditor or a restaurant contractor. You may think that you will remodel for $50,000 and you really have to remodel for $500,000. I have a restaurant for sale now, and one of the problems is that the sewer system keeps clogging up, you know, it's a septic tank. Malibu doesn't have an underground sewer system. We've had contractors go out. The cheapest bid that we got, which was under-bid, was $50,000. The top notch guy was $150,000. So, besides just typical remodeling, you may have to pay $150,000 just for the septic tank system.

Interviewer: *You mentioned something about restaurant expeditors.*

Mario Carron: *There are two kinds of expeditors. One to go through the building and to see what's up to code, what's not up to code, if you want to make changes, will you have to pull permits? A restaurant contractor determines what the restaurant is going to cost you. Realistically, what your eyes tell you. There's a restaurant here in Westlake, and this guy's a professional restaurant owner. Before, it was a nice looking restaurant. He knew when he went in there that he needed to make major changes that cost one million dollars. He totally gutted the place. Those renovations are worth 1 million. People think they're going to go in and spend $250,000. They are dreaming, it's going to be hundreds of thousands.*

Very important in evaluating restaurants are its permits. People want a full liquor license. Many licenses issued within the last 5-7 years have an amazing set of provisions on them. A lot also have sunset provisions. Now, what does that mean? It means that when you open up a new restaurant in certain areas like Hollywood, they give you a license, but the license is good for only 7 years. After that time, the license becomes extinguished. You have to apply for the new license as if no license was ever there before. You're opening the door to possible problems.

Dance permits to certain people are crucial. Within the city of

Los Angeles, you cannot request permission for a dance permit until the escrow closes. What a risk! Say you are opening a restaurant that depends heavily on dance. You have to buy the place first and then request a permit. That's why you need expeditors. You want someone who knows how to deal with the city, but there's a risk involved here. Many old 47 licenses you don't have to serve 50% or more of food. The amount of violations going on with the ABC code is amazing. ABC is shorthanded, so they're not enforcing it. Almost all restaurants that have a full cocktail license, it's really what they call a restaurant license, that's predominantly food. And the violations are amazing. If the city comes in, they could take away the license. They only serve 10% and they may never bother you. On the other hand, they may close you down. What a risk. You need someone who really knows their permits and their license. They need to know dance permits, entertainment permits, and the restrictions on the liquor licenses.

Here's another horror story. I sold a restaurant that never got a conditional use permit because the license had been there forever. You could serve until 2 am. What happened is, there was a homeowners association. They have prevented it from selling liquor until 2am so it is no longer profitable. I've never heard of such a thing, but it happens. Along the entire corridor, if you don't have a CUP (Conditional Use Permit), they can restrict your hours now. This is scary. You need paid professionals when you buy these places. A lawyer, an expeditor, a contractor; all of these things are cheap, because they can avoid a catastrophe. Repairs are crucial. Restaurant equipment more than a few years old is worthless. I've seen some restaurants spending $20,000 a year on repairs. That means everything is falling apart. You are going to have to replace everything. You need a contractor to inspect the building and the equipment. That's another pitfall you have to watch fall. This new one that occurred, that one scared the hell out of me. You need experts today when you open up a restaurant to handle everything. I would never do it on my own.

Interviewer: *What about for sellers? What is the biggest mistake sellers make?*

Mario Carron: *A seller wants all cash. Why? There is big chance that the buyer will fall through, and you are not going to get paid. The seller has several problems. He wants all cash, and he wants a new lease. If he signs the lease, he's still responsible.*

Another horror story. A restaurant in Camarillo I sold when I first got into the business. I get a phone call from a doctor in Encino. He had signed this lease four or five owners previously, but the most recent owner failed to pay. The landlord sued everyone on the lease, including this guy who had been out of the project for five years. This doctor was the only one with deep pockets and had to come up with the money to pay this place off. You want to really get off the lease.

Number two, don't trust the buyer. The buyer may appear to be diligent. You open in escrow, once the posting goes up the buyer has to pay a price. Example, in 2008 we had the recession. I had three deals fall apart because the investors had to forfeit their deposits, because the buyer, when he puts the posting up, he says that this is for sale. This has to be a penalty.

Interviewer: *What are the other mistakes that the sellers make?*

Mario Carron: *I want to know if they have the money to buy it. Many people say, no, but I have investors. So I say, good can I talk to the investors. Most Landlords are pretty tough. They know that if you're a restaurant owner, you may be in trouble. They want someone who is financially strong if they can't pay the rent. Sellers think that if they sell, they walk away with clean hands. Not necessarily true at all. They still may have legal obligations that they would have to worry about.*

Interviewer: *Mario, how do you evaluate the value of a restaurant? What is the best way to do that?*

Mario Carron: *That's a very difficult question. It's not a science, not a computer printout. About ten years ago, I gave a lecture for accountants in continuing education. All of them were pissed off with me. They wanted formulas, but it doesn't work that way in restaurants at all. It only works that way if everything is perfect. The value of the restaurant is in the eye of the beholder. I believe this, I've sent people to restaurants and said, what a lousy restaurant why are you sending me this place? I've got these people in Malibu. She's got a cookbook, she's famous, she has a catering business in Malibu and she's well known, and works in the cable industry and all of that. They just had to have this one location. Now they are willing to pay maybe $250,000. So, how do you evaluate the restaurant? I start by picking a number that I would pay for the place. I know what things sell for.*

Interviewer: *So how do you come up with that number?*

Mario Carron: *I subscribe to the Pacific Report, which costs about $2,000 a year. Anything that enters escrow, the price is published. Every price is confirmed. So, I had an idea. Every single morning I check the embassy website, and I check new applications and licenses there. One third of those that enter escrow are never completed. So, I look at a restaurant based on historical evidence and also the market. I look at what the market has as "in" and what's "out". Most restaurants in L.A. County will never sell. They sell for the price of the liquor license. No buyers, they will never sell. Certain locations have buyers. Right here in Agoura, I have a restaurant for sale. You've got to be able to command a good price, but then even if the location is great, what about the landlord? You may have an impossible lease. You may have license and permit restrictions that kill the value. You've got to look at the condition of the place. Some restaurants you go in and you find that everything needs to go. Right to the walls. So, I take a walk through, I look at the list and say that I would give a number for what I would pay.*

Interviewer: *I am pretty much good with my question. Is there* *anything that I've left out?*

Mario Carron: *Advertising, how I find buyers. I used to spend obscene amounts of money. I used to spend $1,500 with the L.A. Times. I used to spend $3,000 a month on Yellow Pages, today, nothing. Everything today is Internet. I have very powerful Internet sources. I pay a lot of money to advertise via the Internet. Just because I use $3,000 a month doesn't mean I have to sell.*

One last horror story. A really sweet kid. There was a night club on the pier. Net worth was staggering sums of money. He bought it for $350,000 or $450,000. Cash inherited money. Everyone lied including the landlord. I couldn't even sell the place because there is so much mold in the place. They had to close it down. They're suing the broker. This kid had inherited the money. Rags-to-riches in two generations. Could you imagine his family if they were alive? They worked all their lives for this kid to blow their money in 6 months. Thank god his parents are gone. Leaving all of their money to some kid and it's gone in 6 months.

Interviewer: *Thank you so much Mario, this was incredibly valuable and I do thank you so much for your time.*

Interview 2

Rob Baldwin, CLU, CFP, Business Planning and Wealth Transfer Specialist

GBS Insurance and Financial Services

Rob's areas of expertise include estate planning, key person coverage, business succession planning, buy-sell planning, deferred compensation plans, and qualified retirement plans. In 2009, he was awarded the Life Sales and Risk Consultant of the Year Award by Marsh Private Client Services.

Interviewer: *What can happen to a business that waits until it is too late to implement a good business continuation plan?*

Rob Baldwin: *I worked with an ad firm that has 2 partners. Unfortunately, one of the partners developed lung cancer. He was able to treat it and went into remission for a time, but it came back a couple years later. The business had a buy/sell agreement in place, but had not purchased life insurance to fund it. By the time the partner's cancer was diagnosed, it was impossible for him to qualify for life insurance. After his death, the surviving partner had no choice but to sell the business. It was the only way for him to implement the buy/sell agreement.*

Interviewer: *What is the biggest misconception about life insurance?*

Rob Baldwin: *Most people think life insurance is only about the death benefit, but permanent or whole life insurance policies have many benefits available to a policyholder during their lifetime. The cash value of a whole life insurance policy can be used as an "emergency fund" and may offer tax advantages and other advantages over other sources of quick and ready cash.*

Many insurance companies offer riders that allow policyholders to use some of the death benefit while they are still living if, for example, they become terminally ill or need long term care.

Interviewer: *What are some of the tax advantages of life insurance versus other investments?*

Rob Baldwin: *A considerable amount of the Internal Revenue Service is devoted to the tax benefits of life insurance. Some of the major advantages are:*

- *First and foremost death benefits are tax free. This means your beneficiary receives all of the policy amount without paying a single dollar in taxes.*

- *The cash value of a whole life insurance policy grows tax deferred. You do not pay taxes on any gains in the cash value, and when you withdraw from your policy the principal is considered withdrawn first and is tax free.*

- *If you withdraw the entire amount of the cash value of your policy, it is often best to consider any additional withdrawal as a loan against the policy. Loans from a life insurance policy are not taxed as long as the policy stays in force. This is because a loan reduces the amount of the death benefit dollar for dollar. It is akin to getting an "advance" on the death benefit.*

Interviewer: *What are some uses of life insurance policies for business owners?*

Rob Baldwin: *There are many ways in which life insurance can benefit a business and ensure its continuation should one of the owners die. Life insurance can be used to fund a buy/sell agreement. Buy/sell agreements spell out the terms under which a business will be sold or transferred upon death, disability, or retirement of one of the owners. If an owner dies, the life insurance benefit can be used to fund the transfer of ownership to the surviving partner or shareholders.*

Interviewer: *What are some things to consider when executing a buy/sell agreement for my business?*

Rob Baldwin: *The value of your business is going to change over time. It is a good idea to do a valuation at the start of your business and periodically (every 5 years or so) thereafter. Make sure the amount of life insurance you are using to fund the agreement in case of the death of an owner is adequate. Also, remember the buy/sell agreement is not a static document. Be sure to review and update it periodically to reflect any change in the business itself, ownership, etc.*

CHAPTER 9

Valuable Insurance and Risk Management Resources

To View the Resource Links and Websites Please Visit

www.CoopersInsurance.com/bookresources

CAL OSHA website – valuable information about workplace safety and regulations in California.

Spellbound Development Group website - safety and risk management products for various industries.

Shoes for Crews website – slip resistant footwear.

Cut resistant gloves/mitts - a great way to reduce cutting accidents.

Customer Accident/Incident Report Form – to be completed in case of an accident involving a customer.

Cyber Liability/Data Breach checklist – things to consider to make sure your customer's private information is secure.

Payment Card Industry Data Security Standards – detailed credit card processing security requirements and standards.

Personal Property inventory for your home – don't wait until after the incident. Use this inventory to help a homeowner insurance claim go smoothly.

FEMA basic disaster supply kit – be ready when the "big one" hits!

Emergency preparation for your business – what to do when disaster strikes.

Disaster readiness for office, home, car, everywhere

Website of Keith Fink, Esq. – attorney specializing in labor law and expert in employment related matters.

Website of Mario Carron – restaurant broker and expert in buying and selling businesses.

Employee Incident Report – a form to report employee accident and injury.

Safety and Sanitation checklist – make sure your food safety practices are safe and compliant.

Restaurant Loss Prevention Checklist – recognize and correct hazards before a claim can occur!

CHAPTER 10

My Promise to You

- You will have access to my 28 years of experience and expertise in the commercial restaurant insurance industry.

- You will receive outstanding service regardless of the size of your restaurant and your business.

- I will never take your business for granted.

- I will be there when you need me.

- I am an affiliate of a top 50 US insurance agency with access to over 150 of the best insurance carriers.

- I will conduct a comprehensive review of your policies and provide recommendations.

- I will be your dedicated broker that will fight for the best renewal policy for you every year and not just initially to get your business.

- A caring staff that strives to exceed your expectations.

- To be an agency that can take care of your restaurant insurance needs including course of construction, bonds, catering, Worker's Compensation, EPLI, Umbrella, Commercial Vehicle, Earthquake, Property Liability Package, Group Health, Disability, Life, Buy-Sell, and your personal insurance.

Our website is designed with you in mind. It is easy to navigate with valuable newsletters and information. Please visit us at www.coopersinsurance.com or use the QR code below for easy access.

Please feel free to contact me personally with any questions or for a one-on-one consultation.

Scott Cooper

Cooper's Insurance Agency

30423 Canwood St., Suite 239

Agoura Hills, CA 91301

Phone (310) 256-2232

Toll-free (800) 973-2292

Email scottc@coopersinsurance.com

Made in the USA
Monee, IL
29 April 2021

67293225R00085